Winning Short Story Competitions

L. E. DANIELS & C. SAWYER

HAWKEYE
PUBLISHING

First published in Australia in 2020 by Hawkeye Publishing.
Copyright © L. E. Daniels & C. Sawyer.

All rights reserved. No part of this book may be reproduced, stored in a retrieval system, or transmitted, in any form or by any means, without the prior permission in writing of the publisher, not be otherwise circulated in any form of binding or cover other than that in which it is published and without a similar condition including this condition being imposed on the subsequent purchaser.

Proudly printed in Australia by SOS.

Printed in 12 font to aid vision impaired readers.

ISBN 978-0-6483661-2-6

www.hawkeyepublishing.com.au
www.hawkeyebooks.com.au

'Write a short story every week. It's not possible to write 52 bad short stories in a row.' *Ray Bradbury.*

CONTENTS

CHAPTER   **PG**

1. How to Impress Judges — 1
2. Behind the Scenes: How One Literary Judge Approaches Short Story Comps — 7
3. Your Writerly Self — 13
4. Hint, Tantalise, Reel Me In — 22
5. Let's Talk Tautologies & Filters — 38
6. Enter Late, Leave Early — 51
7. BFFs: How Dialogue Makes Plot, Theme & Conflict Shine — 57
8. POV: Who's the Boss? — 65
9. The Art of Self-Editing — 77
10. Top Drawer Writing Groups & Peer Review — 98
11. Your Title, Your Promise — 116

Recommended Resources — 119

Ten Weeks of Creative Writing Exercises to Hone Your Skills — 123

FOREWORD

LIKE musicians and painters, writers are collectors. We gather high notes and low notes, and seek truant shades to make our palettes fresh again. What better place to test new sounds and colours but from within the cosmos of short stories?

Short fiction is in demand. For emerging writers, it's a swift path to publication—swifter than that first novel, for sure. Submission calls are global and a few publications will light up the published portfolio when we're ready to pitch a first book. Listing with a competition conveys to publishers that we can follow guidelines, work with editors, and gather an audience—the star qualities they seek. We'll also have something sweet to share on our social media pages and online profiles to cultivate an audience.

By length, the three types of short fiction are:

Micro-Fiction—up to 100 words

Hemingway's 'Baby Shoes' haunts me with feelings of inadequacy. How did he do this? 'For sale. Baby shoes. Never worn.' There are loads of comps for micro.

Flash Fiction—100 – 1,000/1,500 words

Flash makes great practice, with reams of flash fiction submission calls for emerging writers.

Short Story—1,000/1,500 – 7,500 words (and sometimes up to 10,000)

Periodicals, anthologies, and web-based zines seek longer, traditional short stories. Publishing a few of these will make the first book easier to take to market.

Over the years, Cate and I have collectively judged many competitions and have seen what makes stories dance. Our goal for this book is to make our experience and insight accessible to writers who want to write well, regardless of their levels of education.

If any literary advice covered in this book proves challenging, please follow up with further study, or feel free to contact us.

The elements explored through these pages take time to absorb.

Structure

A true short story is fiction. It needs a literary arc—rising action to climax to falling action. The taut focus is propelled by conflict from hook to resolution. The start and finish form a mirror somehow, to heighten cohesion and sharpen our message. We'll consider ways to enhance structure through technique and an array of literary elements.

Scene

Good stories have tangible scenes that sparkle with sensory imagery. Precise details push the plot and illuminate theme. Literary devices stitch moments together and draw them alive. Exposition and backstory serve as measured intrusions on dramatic action as transitions glide readers from scene to scene toward the climax or an absurd, but earned, unravelling. Readers want to fall into a dream as a story unfolds, so how do we writers tiptoe without waking them?

Characterisation

A controlled cast serves a short story. Anton Chekhov demonstrated that the greatest power lies between two people intersecting. Authentic characters 1.) transform, or 2.) refuse to transform at a cost, and 3.) reveal truth. So how can we make our cast serve the story, and not the other way around?

Style

From the precision of Hemingway to the levitations of Woolf, stylistic choices craft the stature of our stories. *For heaven's sake* and *at the end of the day*, we cut clichés and use our own words. Readers want something new from us, so let's deliver it.

Message

Theme runs like a golden thread—fresh, subtle, and universal. Art points to something larger than itself. Who are we as writers and what we are trying to say is just as important as our technique.

Resonance

Good stories echo within readers for years. 'Strong Horse Tea' by Alice Walker leaves us muddy and stricken. Henry Lawson's 'The Loaded Dog' lingers with the smell of explosives. Writers have hearty egos and strive to leave an impression—a touch of perfume or scratches on the wall. What's yours like?

L. E. Daniels

CHAPTER ONE

HOW TO IMPRESS JUDGES

By C. Sawyer

WE writers are a bold bunch. When we enter competitions, we're pitting ourselves against a legion of other writers who are largely just as talented and passionate about their subject as we are. Competitions are filled with good to great writers.

The difference between winners and the well-populated layer of the field that score around the 8/10 mark for their work, is that winners dedicate time to learning the comprehensive craft of writing, and they've written about their topic in their unique voice. Their writing is original and filter free. Their love of words leaps from the page. Not in a grandstanding way—some writers use words just to show how smart they are. Brilliant writers use words to catapult their reader inside the action. Their reader is so close to the action they *become* the character.

As a judge, it's stunning to read and judge entry after entry, thinking, 'Most of these are quite good, how am I ever going to choose one single entry as the winner?'

On occasion, there are two to four entries that *could* all be the winner, and the judges start the tough process of choosing only one. In extreme circumstances, the difference between the first and second place could be as minor as the winner followed the guidelines and submitted their story in 1.5 line spaced format with Times New Roman (as asked), whereas the second place writer didn't. Don't be the goat who could have won but didn't because they got lazy just before they crossed the finish line!

Why you might like to listen to us:

L. E. Daniels directs the Brisbane Writers Workshop and is a qualified editor, author and mentor. She has a Master of Fine Arts, Creative Writing from Emerson College in Boston USA, and a Bachelor of Arts, Creative Writing from Fairfield University USA. Daniels is sought after as a literary judge, since 2004. She has edited 90+ commercially published books and runs a series of writing workshops for fiction and non-fiction writers.

C. Sawyer directs Hawkeye Publishing and Hawkeye Books. She is a publisher, editor, author and presenter. She has a Master of Arts Writing through Swinburne University, Melbourne, Australia. The former Newspaper Editor has a published portfolio spanning 30 years. She mentors writers on

Show Not Tell, The Art of Self-Editing, and Winning Short Story Competitions. Sawyer is a literary judge for short story and book manuscript competitions.

A Taste of What's to Come—The Winning Formula:

Whilst we can't guarantee you a first place—that's up to you, your imagination, and your creative skills—we can guarantee that *without* these essential criteria covered, substantial writing prizes will stay out of reach.

1. Practise, practise, practise the art of Show Not Tell. The difference between a page-turner and a sleeper, is that a writer has mastered this essential writing element. Use the five senses to place the reader in the story. Good writers spend their entire careers improving this tool. It's easy to read Anton Chekhov's famous quote, 'Don't tell me the moon is shining, show me the glint of light on broken glass,' and think you've 'got it'. Dig deeper. There's much to learn on this topic.

2. Enter the story as late as you can, and leave as early as you can. This minimises the risk of a slow start that doesn't grab your reader, and killing the ending with too much description.

3. Create credible, three dimensional characters who are flawed.

4. Write authentic dialogue. Real people rarely talk in well-rounded, fully-formed sentences in actual speech.

5. Ensure that your characters have differing voices/personalities. You should be able to strip away your speech tags (i.e., Kitty said, Fletcher said), read your story out loud, and have your audience know who said what. If they can't, draw more character nuances and speech patterns into the prose.

6. Work on your story's structure and pace. Your story must have a beginning that grabs, rising action, i.e., inciting incidents that build tension, a climax, and a resolution. Longer sentences slow the pace, so curate shorter sentences to build tension.

7. Ensure your main character is an instigator of action. Passive bystanders reacting to events are boring. Strong characters take action.

8. If you need an adverb/verb combination to say what one strong verb can say, you've chosen the wrong verb. Choose strong, interesting verbs. Explore verbs. Enjoy them—they make all the difference. One well-placed verb can often replace half a sentence. Looking at a thesaurus to replace a word in your text is not enough.

9. Remove redundant words. We all litter our first drafts with overwritten text. For example, 'Sawyer began to giggle'. No, just no. 'Sawyer giggled' has more

dramatic impact. Learn all you can about redundant words (filters) and slash them from your drafts. As you practise editing them out, your first-draft writing improves.

10. Proofreading a short story is far easier than a novel. Errors are amateurish in a short story competition. Ensure correct spelling, grammar, punctuation and formatting.

11. And last, but by no means least, don't be a goat! Read the competition guidelines and any theme requirements and abide by them. In some competitions, your entry won't even be read if you haven't conformed to the submission guidelines. If you haven't bothered, why should they? Writers sometimes submit pre-written stories to themed competitions. Their story doesn't acknowledge the theme, but they consider their writing is brilliant and they'll win anyway. They won't.

It's easy to read the above list and assume knowledge. In the following chapters, we explore these themes in detail and offer illustrative examples. Surface assumption of knowledge stifles your learning practice, closing doors on unrealised potential. Allow for the a-ha moments in the coming chapters. Congratulations on your growth mindset. You're a step ahead.

Winning competitions is terrific. It gives you an incredible boost of enthusiasm to drive your regular writing practice. Whether you win, short or long list in writing competitions, you're endorsed to have the skills and talent of a career writer.

CHAPTER TWO

BEHIND THE SCENES: HOW ONE LITERARY JUDGE APPROACHES SHORT STORY COMPS

By L. E. Daniels

MANY of the competitions I've judged had at least 60 entrants, mostly from Australia with a few European, North American, Asian and New Zealand writers in the running too. Several of the contests routinely had more than double that number of entries, so it can be a process to produce long and short lists, then determine the winners.

It's an honour to be asked to read and rank manuscripts for these competitions. I know it takes guts to write and even more to enter our work into a competition. I bear that in mind with each page I touch.

To share some insight on how I rank stories, I employ five technical approaches plus one added category, resonance, which is less technical but just as pivotal. Cited in the foreword, these approaches are explored further here and maybe it helps to dig into this at the start and we'll unpack some points further in the coming chapters.

Structure & Focus

When I first look at a story, I assess its contours. I want to see how it all sticks together or if it falls apart. This may be my first culling measure because if the writing rambles, breaks into tangents, and doesn't have a central axis guiding the experience, it's not a story; it's a sketch. A strong focus supported by literary structure makes a great short story. So here's what I ask first.

Does the story have an expression of the literary arc—rising action to climax to falling action? If the story is experimental and breaks from traditional structure, does it have a strong focus from start to finish?

Is there a hook that draws readers into the opening scene? Polished openers with immediate lift-off make strong impressions.

Do the start and end form a link—a mirror or connection of sorts between the two moments? An image, a mood, an object or even a colour laced into both the open and close of a story can add that extra bit of writerly intention—a powerful ingredient.

Departures from a chronological ordering of scenes can also provide energy to the structure. Perhaps the author uses a frame—where the beginning and the end are conveyed from the same time or voice—to strengthen cohesion. Writers can also start from a moment close to the climax, then return to the start to grab readers and fill them in on what they need to know later, a classical technique called *in medias res*. Does the writer show creativity in how the story unfolds?

Lastly, how do the conflict and stakes empower the focus and structure of the story? Does conflict drive the narrative, coupled with a surprise at the three-quarters mark or at the end? The best stories have an escalating sense of drama readers can trust.

Scenes & Transitions

Next, I observe the scenes and the movement, or transitions, between them. The best stories have tangible scenes drawn alive through the senses and precise detail that reflect and develop the core theme. Scenes are highlighted by literary devices which, like tone, symbolism, or motif, can act as stitching for the story.

A good story shows its events more than tells them, so I measure how much exposition or backstory intrudes on the dramatic action. Are we given enough information without breaking up the pace? Or does the dramatic action flat line into a large paragraph of information, dumped for the reader to digest? Economy is crucial in short stories, so I observe the efficiency and precision of the scene work.

As I read across the scenes, I consider transitions. Do we move seamlessly from scene to scene and do I get a sense of gravity as we move toward the climax? Or do I get jarred from the story as I lose my footing? Like most readers, I don't want to be kicked out of the story from confusion or jagged edges. I want to stay right where the author wants me—focused on the dream of the story.

Characterisation

Let's assess the size of the cast. Poorer quality stories have too many characters and stronger ones have a limited cast. In some stories, the greatest power can ignite between two characters and the magnetic or repellent energy between them. This intersection illuminates conflict and theme as the energy of a story is released to the reader.

Authenticity beats cliché, so I assess how dimensional and unique the characters appear or if they are flat and predictable. How do the characters express themselves—is it memorable or forgettable? Do they feel like people I could know or are they like clay golems, still amorphous and emerging from the draft?

When the characters speak, I ask if they all sound the same and if there are clichés in their dialogue. Clichés can work in dialogue—sparingly—if they point to a character's background or add a touch of humour, but readers don't want a predictable, *one trick pony*.

Lastly, I ask how the characters evolve and assess the character arc. Do the characters experience challenges and some form of transformation? If they resist transformation, is there a cost? If they are static, unchanging characters, is the story about their integrity in a challenging world and what does that say about them?

Characters are crucial to a short story's credibility. I'll ask: Do we believe in these people? Can we follow them into this dream?

Style

Stylistic choices and voice are critical elements contributing to the stature of a piece of writing. A solid voice and defined presence invite both the trust and imagination of the reader.

Are there conscious word choices and turns of phrase that do not rely on cliché, but rather embody the voice of the author? Is it confident and consistent, or is it timid and in flux?

Elmore Leonard wrote in his 2001 *New York Times* article, 'Easy on the Adverbs, Exclamation Points and Especially Hooptedoodle': 'If it sounds like writing, I rewrite it'. That belongs on a sticky note at our writing desks.

Message

Every work of art has a message. I explore what the work means, its inherent question, and the theme grappled by the characters and the narrator.

Is the author conveying a meaningful theme that runs like a golden thread from start to finish? Is it fresh? Is it subtle or overt? Is it gentle or didactic? Does the author trust the reader's insight and experience, or is it overwritten, with little left to intuit?

Good art is not just evocative; it is also collective. Is there a glance of universal truth? Does the work point to something larger than itself?

It seems to me that all the good stories urge readers to feel something and to have their worldviews grown, somehow, by the experience of the story. Like many readers, if I am challenged and left wondering about the world and my beliefs, I appreciate the work on a wider scale.

A story with a message doesn't equate literary snobbery, either. Even an urban fantasy about vampires or a wartime bodice ripper can leave readers questioning their perceptions. That's the good stuff.

Resonance

Narrowing things down into lists and ranks can get a bit tricky, so this last category was added as I became a more experienced judge.

When I review my long and short lists, I notice if rereading the first page stirs an echo within me; if the writing left a strong sense of itself, like an imprint. I see this impression as a culmination of a writer's skills and it takes distinct, directed energy to create a profound response in readers.

A story's resonance ventures into the transcendent territory of the arts, but most readers know what I mean. When a story leaves its fingerprints on us, it's unmistakable. We feel it.

Sometimes coming up with a clear winner comes right down to the implicit energy of a lasting impression.

CHAPTER THREE

YOUR WRITERLY SELF

By C. Sawyer

PUBLISHED authors never stop learning and developing the craft. I beta read for international bestselling author, Kylie Kaden (currently Pantera Press). Her debut novel, *Losing Kate*, is a page-turner. I *loved* it. I recently beta read her fourth novel and was spellbound to see how much her writing had developed between her first and fourth books; and this from an already exceptional author. Everyone, no matter who we are, the more we write, the better we become. And not only is our growth as a writer personally rewarding, it can be financially rewarding.

I was first commercially published in 1987. I've been a newspaper editor, and now an author, book editor, publisher and a writing competition judge. I'd like to share something that might surprise some. I still attend writing courses, manuscript critique groups and writing conferences, and I hire a structural editor and line editor for the books I author. Kylie Kaden attends with me a social networking group for published authors. Writing is not a solitary journey.

Some writers think they should bang away on their computers and hide their work to ensure their brilliant idea isn't stolen. Then they think they'll send their perfect story to top tier publishers and competitions and overnight, watch the competition wins, literary awards and mega-buck royalties roll in. They're wrong.

The 'overnight success stories' one hears ... of authors going viral and securing huge advances ... are the result of authors chipping away for years, just like everyone else, before they achieve success.

Unless you're writing for self-healing and your eyes only, writing is not a solitary pursuit. It involves readers, plural.

Writing is not a Solitary Journey

On top of your love of words and your enjoyment in crafting delightful sentences, I cannot encourage you enough to leave the safety of your desk to seek and give meaningful feedback on writing. You'll find that networking:
1. Inspires you and the energy is infectious.
2. Opens your mind to new opportunities.
3. Expands your knowledge about the technique and business of writing.

4. Introduces you to people that know how to get published.

Attend Writing Conferences

Amy Andrews, an award-winning, *USA Today* best-selling Aussie author with 70+ books and over 3 million copies sold, once said to me, 'The best piece of advice I can give you is to attend your genre's annual industry conference and when you're there, work it; network it 'til the death, the people in that room ... you'll never find them altogether anywhere else.'

I didn't heed her advice immediately—I was busy and conferences aren't cheap. But then I attended the Children Young Adult Conference in Brisbane and ... mind blown. The workshops and panels were high level. I met ragingly successful authors and added them to my circle. And perhaps the most valuable opportunity of all, I was able to pitch my manuscripts to publishers. Fifteen-minute pitching sessions to publishers are now the norm at industry conferences and they're an invaluable opportunity. I paid for the privilege and received immediate feedback. This instant insight into the mindset of publishers regarding my story concept was galvanising.

Join a Writing Group

Whilst I'm an advocate for the benefits of attending writing conferences, they can be expensive. For a free space to give and receive writing feedback, join a writing group. There are many around and your library or state writing centre can point to those nearby. If you attend a meeting and it doesn't feel right, try another. Not every group's structure and the personalities of those in attendance, will suit you; but one will. Visit groups as a guest until you find the right fit. Peer support is invaluable in terms of critiquing and learning opportunities. It's not only about what you can gain from the group, equally important is what you can contribute to others—give and take—it's an evocative dance and your efforts will be remembered when it matters.

If, like me, the group you're seeking isn't available nearby; start the group you have in mind. I put a call out on social media and through my state writing centre, for published authors to get together once a month for an industry guest speaker, friendship, and professional peer support. I phoned local libraries and was offered a free meeting room to use once a month. Brisbane Book Authors is now in its fifth year.

In most writing groups, you'll have the opportunity to share your work with other writers who can critique from a learned space—as opposed to your mum or best friend who can critique on whether or not they enjoyed the piece. Fellow writers can offer constructive feedback on structure, pace, tense, beginning, middle, and ends, adverbs, redundant words, scene setting, characterisation, dialogue. Sharing your work in a writing group offers you the opportunity to see your work from a knowledgeable reader's perspective. You'll see what lands well, and what doesn't work the way you thought it might.

A word of caution about feedback on your work; a good critique partner knows that it is equally important to highlight the gems in your story, as the areas that need work. Writers learn as much from knowing what resonates with the beta reader, as we do by seeing what doesn't.

Some feedback on your writing will sting, but with practise you'll put it into perspective. You will come across writers who give excellent constructive feedback. You will also encounter those who simply offer their own personal likes and dislikes—another reason why a group space for feedback can be beneficial. If one person gives you feedback that you oppose, you can choose whether you take on their advice. However, if three or four people tell you the same thing ... well, you might take heed.

Sharing your writing in a group isn't all about having tough skin. Every time I interact with fellow authors, I come away enthused, inspired, raring to go on that section that's proving troublesome. I love the energy that authors exude. They share my passion and hanging with them *always* puts a smile on my face. I share my triumphs with peers who appreciate how much work it took, and I laugh at the ridiculousness of what we do with those who 'get it'.

In writing groups, we learn from each other, and guest speakers. We're energised by our peers' enthusiasm. And we hear of opportunities—competitions, submission calls, fellowships, worthwhile courses, whose professional editing someone was happy or not happy with—that otherwise might escape us.

Attend Courses and Read Books (Like this one—kudos to you!)

Actively learn to develop your craft. Our industry is ever evolving, and so should you ever evolve as a writer.

Our libraries offer good courses for free. In Australia, our libraries are an exceptional resource that we're lucky to have. (I would like to hear from readers from other countries about your libraries). There are also many excellent fee-based short courses to attend, like the Brisbane Writers Workshop and Queensland Writers Centre near me. I learn something new at every course I attend.

I'm often asked, 'Will doing a degree in writing make me a better writer?' I certainly don't regret doing my Master of Arts Writing. It gave me the confidence to speak the speak and backed up my professionalism as a Communications Consultant and Editor. However, if someone asked me if they *needed* to do a degree to be a better short story writer, I'd answer, 'Degrees, whilst excellent, are an extraordinary financial and time investment.'

On the other hand, short courses offer exceptional opportunities to improve your writer's tool bag in manageable bursts. All writers should study show not tell, strong verbs, story structure, point of view, self-editing, giving and receiving beta reader feedback. There are good short courses readily available in all of these topics, and you'll find many excellent books on writing by reputable authors. Writers also learn exponentially by hiring a professional editor—consider this an excellent spend of education funds.

Be an Active Member of Your Professional Association

I recommend being a member of your professional associations. I'm a member of Queensland Writers Centre, Australian Society of Authors and the Alliance of Independent Authors. You'll get professional newsletters with industry news, inspiring articles, and competitions and opportunities. You'll be informed and up-to-date, and you'll be supporting professional organisations that are supporting us. Many also offer good discounts with trading partners, e.g., by being a member of the Alliance of Independent Authors I get free uploads onto Ingram Spark. It proves worthwhile.

Read

Many writers quote Stephen King's *On Writing* as their favourite book. There's good reason ... his joy for writing rubs off. I spent twenty years saying I was going to write a book one day. I read *On Writing*, and the draft of my first book was completed 12 months later.

In the words of King, 'If you want to be a writer you must do two things above all others: read a lot and write a lot. We need to experience the mediocre and outright rotten; such experience helps us to recognise such things when they creep into our own work. We've all heard someone say "man, it was great (or hard, or strange, or funny). I just can't describe it." If you want to be a successful writer, you must be able to describe it, and in a way that will cause your reader to prickle with recognition.'

King says he is floored when he hears someone wants to be a bestselling writer, but they don't have time to read books themselves. How can you possibly know what is unique, superb, and current, if you're not reading in your genre?

Write

Would you like to know the difference between writers I know who are published, and writers I know who aren't? Wanna-be-published writers dream of one day having a solid block of time to write their book without interruption. On the other hand, published authors have a daily writing practice.

Chunk it down. No matter how busy you are, if writing is in your blood, you can write 500 words a day. Five hundred words doesn't take long, and if prioritised, you can do it at least five days a week. Five hundred words, five days a week is 2,500 words per week. In 26 weeks, that writer has the first draft of a 65K word book.

Need more inspiration? One of Australia's bestselling indie romance authors, Rachael Amphlett, wrote her first books on the train commuting to and from work—I know this because she was an enthralling guest speaker at Brisbane Book Authors.

If you want to win short story competitions … commit to writing one 1,000-word short story per week and watch how much your writing improves. That's only 200 words a day.

Submit your best works to competitions. And write to

us and tell us what it feels like the first time you see your name in print!

To Recap, My Recommendations for Your Writerly Self:

1. Join a writing group.
2. Attend writing courses.
3. Be an active member in your professional organisation/s.
4. Attend your genre specific conferences.
5. Read.
6. Write—commit to an easily achievable, Monday to Friday daily word count. Make writing your habit.

CHAPTER FOUR

HINT, TANTALISE, REEL ME IN

By C. Sawyer

SHOW don't tell advice is thrown around writing groups and courses like confetti. Truth is, there is a time and place for both show and tell, especially in short stories.

If anything important happens in your story, it has to be related dramatically; via a scene told in real time with your characters moving about—talking, acting, reacting and feeling; experiencing events moment by moment. Those scenes are always shown not told.

However, if there is no value to the plot/tension/conflict/character arc by showing mundane but necessary information, showing will slow the story. In these instances, telling is preferable.

Memorable writing results from the right balance.

EXAMPLE 1

TELL: My stepdad, Jack, beats me.

One would surmise this is most likely an important event in the evolution of Jack, so we want the reader to 'feel' it. Therefore, we'd 'show' it.

SHOW:

'You're a miscreant!' a menacing figure hovering over me shouts.
It's my stepdad, Jack. He always uses big words, even at church meetings, so people can admire him as more of a man of God.
Whack!
'You're an ingrate!'
Whack! Whack!
'You have no respect for your parents!'
Whack! Whack! Whack!
(Excerpt from *Shriek: an absurd novel* by Davide A. Cottone).

EXAMPLE 2

Consider that in an upcoming scene, the cold rain is important because when your character walks into the heated room of her attacker, she's at a disadvantage because her senses are dulled by her heavy clothing and stiffened limbs. We want our reader to feel the lead-up.

TELL: The motorbike sped through the pelting rain.

SHOW: Burrowed under full leathers, crystals of ice on her gloves stiffened her fingers as the wind slapped rain into her body. She gunned the bike, trying to outrun the cold.

The 'show' example evokes emotion in our readers; they 'feel' the cold.

However, let's say you want to show a changing location and time, but your arc is centred squarely on what happens at the next location, you might write, 'In the morning, she knocked on Nicholas' door…' Then revert to show for the next important character arc scene.

Telling is factual, brief, and efficient. It avoids detail and conveys broad overarching messages such as 'it was winter'. Telling does not, in general, stir the heart.

Showing is slower, richer, more expansive. It is not efficient; it loves the detail. Showing tends to describe the manifestation of some or all of the senses and often stirs the heart.

To improve our own sensitivity to vivid, suggestive sense impressions, cultivate the habit of trying to identify—as you go through your normal everyday activities—the dominant impressions you receive at any given moment.

Showing is particularly relevant for fiction, because in fiction we don't explain; we hint to tantalise and engage. However, writers who have mastered 'show' and incorporate this into their non-fiction writing offer their readers a far more satisfying read than a dry story.

What is Showing?

1. Don't explain—hint.
2. Present stimuli, and involve, convince, and excite readers by allowing them to draw their own conclusion through the stimuli presented.
3. For readers to immerse themselves in the experiences of characters, they need to feel them as the characters themselves feel them.
4. Your character experiences sense impressions and everything else moment by moment; briefly, often in a fragmented manner, and vividly because it's the real world they are experiencing.

How to 'Show':

1. Use the character's five senses.
2. Use strong verbs.
3. Minimise adverbs.
4. Be specific.
5. Use dialogue.

6. Focus on actions and reactions.
7. Close your eyes and picture yourself doing what the character is doing. What do you notice first? What can you see, smell, hear, feel, taste?
8. Present those impressions as vividly and briefly as possible in a logical order.
9. Boil your words down to reflect real life sense perception and make the words you choose as vivid and evocative as possible.

EXAMPLE 3:

Instead of telling, 'I realised I loved him,' describe how the feeling manifested and let your invested reader infer that this was the moment she realised she loved him. Readers are intelligent and enjoy working out the ahas.

e.g., SHOW I realised I loved him:

My leg sat millimetres from his, tortuously close. The long anticipated movie mere background noise; all my senses finely attuned to his nearness, my skin tingling. He moved and his fingers brushed mine. A flush burned my cheeks. The beginnings of a smile formed, belying my fear at being vulnerable to another human.

Revealing Characters

The same principle of show not tell applies when it comes to showing your readers your other story characters. You could lecture your readers and tell them Sawyer is nervous and impatient. Or evoke their senses by showing.

EXAMPLE 4:

Sawyer's gangly legs walked jerkily into the office. A facial tic leaped under his left eye. He swooped onto the empty chair, drummed his fingers on the desktop, crossed his legs, and glared at me.

'All right. I'm here. I don't have all day. Get to the point.' He couldn't stop his upper lip spasming.

Sitting opposite, I focused my gaze on his disloyal lip. Sawyer shifted in his seat.

Good Practice:

1. When editing your first draft, highlight any basic sensory words, such as I heard, I felt, I tasted, I smelled, I saw. These are all telling words and they act as filters in the storytelling. Rewrite those sentences to show how those feelings manifested without the filter.
2. Highlight any emotion explaining words such as happy, excited, sad, angry, frustrated, scared, love, anxious, and nervous. They're all respectable words

but they're also weak and unexciting. Instead of writing, 'I was angry,' show the emotion building.
3. Check that your dialogue is realistic, and shows a character's state of being so that you don't have to 'tell' the reader who your characters are. To show that Lisa is confused, your dialogue might be, 'What? Say that again.' As opposed to tell, 'Lisa was confused and asked Gerard to repeat the direction.'

Show Examples:

>Her heart scrambled: so fast it felt slow, so hard it churned into liquid. Flames spread, searing everything. Dust swarmed her mouth, speckled her eyes. Her breath startled the air in thin washes. Askew on the ground, she no longer saw the serpent but felt its cold heat.
>(From *Serpent's Wake: A Tale for the Bitten* by L. E. Daniels).

>The tickticktick of terror time slowed into the tick … tick … tick … of focused time.
>(From *Serpent's Wake: A Tale for the Bitten* by L. E. Daniels).

Common Mistake:

Writers often provide information dumps to tell us what their characters are like, e.g., physical characteristics, family background, emotional state, etc. Info dumps bog down the action, often at the story's commencement—prime space to hook the reader. It is far more satisfying when a writer brings a character to life dramatically, through what they say and do, throughout the story. Show not tell overcomes info dumps by concentrated effort on moving the story forward using dialogue and incidents rather than narration.

To further our exploration of Show Not Tell, consider this next scene. The Tell version of these unfolding events would be: Recently widowed Evie Attwater was summoned to the school where her daughter was accused of criminally bullying another female student. But Evie knew, without a doubt, that it was some kind of stitch-up. Her daughter was covering for someone else.

Example of Show Utilising Dialogue and Action:

Evie disconnected the call from her mother-in-law, leant back into the worn leather of Max's favourite chair, and looked longingly at the photo of their little family on the desk. His mother felt his loss just as much as she did. *(Show 'recently widowed').*

Her phone buzzed. The message brief; a summons to school but not with the usual, 'She's fine, we're taking care of her, just come when you can'. This time, 'There's been an incident with Keeta. It's imperative that you come immediately.'

She arrived at the school's reception. Evie noted

the receptionist's furtive look. She couldn't look her in the eye. *Oh God, this IS going to be bad*, thought Evie. *What have they done to my baby girl?* A recently viewed current affairs program foremost in her mind – an interview with parents of a teenager who'd suicided because of high school bullying.

The door opened and Evie caught her first glimpse of Keeta. She faltered mid-step then reached for her pale daughter. Drawing Keeta out of the chair, she wrapped her arms protectively around her only child.

Keeta remained stiff, arms hanging by her side, a prisoner in a hug she didn't acknowledge.

Evie held onto her daughter's hands, stepped back a pace so she could look at her face.

Keeta averted her head. A stubborn set to her jaw and defiant eyes, belied by the red flush on her face and hunched shoulders.

'What's happened, Keeta?' Before Keeta could reply, Evie felt the pressure of the Principal's hand on her right shoulder.

'Mrs Attwater, sit please.'

With her mother's embrace loosened, Keeta slumped back into her chair, uncharacteristic insolence seething in her small frame.

Evie sat. She noted that Keeta angled herself away from the Principal.

'I'm afraid Keeta has got herself in a spot of trouble, and we've had to call the Police. They should be here shortly.'

'What?'

'Keeta has sent naked photos of another female student around to her classmates.'

Evie's head jerked to the side. She looked at her daughter.

'It appears Keeta has been bullying another student, and this morning has escalated that bullying into criminal activity. I've confiscated her phone, and it will be handed to the Police when they arrive.'

'I ... no, that can't be ...,' Evie said. 'Who are you saying she's bullied?'

'At this stage, I'm not at liberty to say. I suggest we wait for the Police to arrive. They can advise how much information can be disclosed to you. The victim's parents are on their way in now.'

Evie's eyes darted from her daughter to the principal, noting Keeta's laboured breathing. Keeta held her mother's gaze, lips parted. But then her mouth closed and she looked away. Evie's mind raced to understand her daughter's body language. And why on earth wouldn't the Principal tell her who was involved?

Consider how much you learned about each of the characters through their speech and actions. You've been told no description of the principal, but I bet you have a vivid picture of him in your mind...

TIP

First drafts are for getting the story onto the page; the writer's imagination unfettered. Don't censor yourself by over-editing as you write. After you've written your first draft, then highlight words/phrases that can be improved. Over time, the more you self-edit, better writing technique will flow into your first draft sentences. It takes time for new skills to flow naturally into your writing.

The first draft is your time to allow your story freedom. Editing is phase two. And learning is continuous.

Lastly, for our dive into Show Not Tell, I'll leave you with the winning short story from the Sydney Hammond Memorial Short Story Competition 2019, themed 'Diversity in Australia'. Note the choice of strong verbs and nouns that show us so much, reel us into the story ... make us feel. Like the choice of 'attack' in the sentence, 'strident sounds all around attack her flesh'. Consider how well the story narrative addresses the competition's theme. It would be a worthwhile exercise to study what the author has chosen to show, and tell, and consider why.

NEW GIRL

By Christine Johnson

*(Past Winner
Sydney Hammond Memorial Short Story Competition)*

NEW girl comes from a war-torn place. Her arrival, refugee rural re-settlement. Everyone knows that.

What they don't know is she thinks of her past as if sitting in an oasis, a garden with men, women and children lying under the palms. These ghosts lying in the shade are all that remain. Confronted by the rubble of a destroyed city, months in a crowded camp and now shifted into foreign, rustic emptiness, she clings to them.

At school she turns up wearing the standard checked uniform dress. The giveaway is the scarf wrapped around her head. She stands at the front of the classroom. The teacher waits until fidgeting stops. Students chant the ritual, 'Good morning, Mrs Bates.'

'This is Amani.' Mrs Bates' eyes scan the room. 'In coming days let's make her welcome.'

Murmurs ripple as the new girl approaches her desk. The backpack strapped to her body attracts nudges - *bomb rather than packed lunch?*

The lesson starts. Freed from the threat of focus, she retreats; swims back and steps ashore in her private haven. She takes her place with the others, lying under the trees.

When the recess bell jangles, out everyone spills from their desks, jostling into the sun-drenched yard. Boys forge ahead. Greg's cockerel laugh leads his mob, their massed breaking voices sounding like cracked china. Clever Tracy emerges next, surrounded by her coterie of girlfriends.

New girl arrives last. Hesitates. Strident sounds all around attack her flesh. She finds a spot to sit alone, at a distance on the library steps. Her shadow sits with her, the colour of a bruise, leaking uncertainty.

Tracy and her coterie approach. Greg and his mates follow.

'Did you see lots killed?'

'Greg!' This is Tracy.

The argumentative words fall close, like an exchange of bullets.

Tracy takes charge, her tone permeated with sympathy. 'Were you frightened?'

The question baffles. Sometimes in her dreams Amani breathes an air so dense with groans and strangled sobs it reaches out and chokes her.

Greg interrupts. 'Hey,' he says, pointing at the headscarf, 'Do you wear that to bed?'

The boys laugh. A tussle and skirmish of assumptions follow.

'Will you have an arranged marriage?'

'Or work? Study at university?'

'How come you got away? Here, to our country?'

At this point Amani's heart beats faster while her blood freezes, wishing to run backwards, to avoid the pain at her centre. How to imagine so many who have died? Let alone understand why she is not amongst them.

She will never forget one old man. Thin legs and the threadbare coat he wore made him seem an ancient bird with fraying feathers. He came wobbling along the laneway on his rusty bike, heading for the main street. Crouched outside her ruined house in what remained of her doorway, terror beating like trapped wings in her belly, she should have stepped forward to warn him. But thumping fear demanded she survive. So, she watched. Sensing the rumble, he falters, and looks up—too late. A lorry full of soldiers travelling at speed smashes into him. The bike buckles. His body flies up, crushed. His brains spill onto the road.

After plying new girl with questions that never receive answers, most shrug, give up. A month passes.

'Hello.'

New girl looks up, startled. The other girl grins, eyes crinkling at the corners, dimple-craters in her suntanned cheeks.

'Can I sit with you?' She does anyway. 'You new?'

'Sort of. Yes.'

'Yeah, me too. First day.'

Amani glances at her. 'From overseas?'

The other girl laughs. 'Not me. Naradhan, know where that is?'

'No.'

'Yeah, well. Neither does anyone else.'

The two chew sandwiches, eyes gazing at the drought-dry oval. The other girl breaks the silence.

'So, what do you play?'

Amani's brows arch, questioning.

'Sport,' the other girl grins.

'Nothing...' She sees the grin fading. 'Except ...'

'Yeah?'

In the camp, a coach came. She trained us. Soccer.'

'Awesome!'

'Yes, the soccer team with girls. I liked that.'

'Girls' soccer—even better! Hey, what's your name?'

'I'm Amani.'

'I'm Samantha. Call me Sam.'

Sam arrives next day with the black-and-white ball. Amani looks at it and remembers a similar ball rolling over rough ground an entire world away.

She recalls bare feet racing on gravel. That, and cheap plastic sandals caught up in hot pursuit. One girl plays in socks. Another manages one-legged, on a crutch. Screams swell from the sidelines after a goal and then fade back into a chorus of urge-on chants. The ball's panels of light and dark breach columns of sunlight and stir up dust motes. The dust dances. Caught up by a hot breeze it whirls, escapes the high wire fencing of the compound; carries up and through all barriers to celebrate wild freedom.

And Amani senses a tingling beneath her skin. She no longer wants to stand in the shadows. When she runs, Sam chases after. They weave and dodge, kicking the ball back and forth. Sometimes they stop, panting, feet apart and hands resting on knees, staring into each other's eyes like animals. No language, but determined to meet. Then the stillness between them breaks into peals of laughter. It rings out as their play continues.

Greg and his mob turn to see who is causing such a row. Tracy and her girlfriends huddle, looking on in amazement. Mrs Bates, on yard duty, strolls across. Greg moves to within earshot.

'Girls playing soccer, it's not right!'

'Why would that be Greg?'

'Footy, it's for boys.'

Mrs Bates gives a rare smile. 'Well, soccer may not cure the entire world's problems, but from what we're seeing here it may shatter certain boundaries.'

By the end of the week what started with two playing soccer has grown—to become the beginnings of an enthusiastic girls' team.

Mrs Bates causes a stir, putting herself forward as coach.

Amani has her first and closest friend, Sam. Inseparable, they do everything together.

(In addition to winning the inaugural Sydney Hammond Memorial Writing Competition, Christine Johnson was shortlisted for the 2017 Alan Marshall Short Story Award, the 2018 Elyne Mitchell Writing Awards and the 2019 Stuart Hadow Prize. Her first full-length novel won the 2019 Eggcellent Manuscript Assessment Competition).

CHAPTER FIVE

LET'S TALK TAUTOLOGIES & FILTERS

By C. Sawyer

TAUTOLOGIES and filters run rampant in first-draft writing. It's not surprising, because early readers at school are filled with them—repetition helps teach word recognition. As adult writers, we must un-learn these sentencing habits and eliminate them because not only do they slow our prose, but they distance the reader from the story. In short stories, their removal frees up precious word count.

Tautology says the same thing in two ways. For example, 'They both turned and looked back,' contains two tautologies. 'They' and 'both' say the same thing when the reader knows there are two characters. 'Turned' and 'back' indicate the same action.

The tautology-free way to write this sentence is, 'They looked back.' That's a 50% saving on the original word count for that sentence.

Filters are unnecessary words that separate the reader from the story's action and make the reader more aware that they are *reading* a scene, rather than *experiencing* one. For example, 'Saul's eyes bulged, and then he ran.' If an action follows another 'then' is implied. The filter-free sentences are 'Saul's eyes bulged. He ran.'

Consider this sentence, the likes of which is often seen in first draft writing:

> He stood at the window and watched her leave and as he did so he felt his heart break.

If we remove the filters it becomes:

> *He stood at the window. She left. His heart broke.*

Feel the difference? Removing the filters catapults a reader inside the action—they're there … in the moment, experiencing it in real time with the character. They *become* the character. And that is when a story is its most powerful.

Tautologies and filters are not your friends—they fill the writing with redundant words. They don't contribute any forward movement or essential information.

Consider these examples of tautologies and filters:

> **FILTER DRIVEN:** I could hear him pack his things and poured myself a vodka and went and sat outside on the back veranda to be out of his way; things were awkward enough already without me gawping at him.

FILTER FREE: A thump, zipper release and shuffling. He packed in record time. His eagerness to leave clocked me in the stomach. Vodka in hand, I settled onto our veranda swing, out of sight, dignity intact.

Common indicators that your sentence/paragraph is filter driven are the inclusion of words such as hear, see, touch, think, wonder, decide, know, feel, notice. There are, of course, more—many more.

Here are simpler examples to break it down:

REDUNDANT: As adults we **must then** un-learn these habits and **consciously** eliminate them **from our** writing because they slow our prose.
BETTER: As adults we un-learn these writing habits and eliminate them because they slow our prose.
(Then is implied. 'From our' is clunky and often un-needed. To 'un-learn' something is a conscious undertaking so 'consciously' is redundant).

REDUNDANT: A tautology **is when we** say the same thing **over again** in two **different** ways.
BEST: A tautology says the same thing in two ways.
('Same thing over again' is a tautology. As is 'two different'. 'Is when we' is a clunky filter).

REDUNDANT: That's a saving **of** 50%.
BETTER: That's a 50% saving.
('Of' is often an un-necessary filter).

REDUNDANT: She was **almost** afraid to open her eyes.
BETTER: She was afraid to open her eyes.
(Almost is rarely needed).

REDUNDANT: John didn't know he **was going to** jump in the river when he saw the kid slip **in**.
BETTER: John didn't know he would jump in the river when he saw the kid slip.
(Passive phrasing like 'was going to' should always be replaced by the active, bolder phrasing. 'In' the river was said earlier in the sentence, so when the child slips it's not necessary to repeat 'in').

REDUNDANT: Tears **were running** down her face.
BETTER: Tears ran down her face.
(Almost always, you should re-phrase passive to active and in so doing filters drop away).

REDUNDANT: Tom's decision was **already** made.
BETTER: Tom's decision was made.
(Decisions are decisive, so already is an un-necessary filter).

REDUNDANT: The energy **was bursting all** around me.
BETTER: The energy burst around me.
(Change passive filter to active verb).

REDUNDANT: Now people are awestruck when they see him.
BETTER: People are awestruck when they see him.
(Are means 'now', making 'now' a tautology here).

REDUNDANT: The lightning **continued to flash all over the place across** the sky.
BETTER: Lightning criss-crossed the sky.
('The' is implied. 'Continued to' is rarely needed. 'Flash all over the place across' is easily replaced by one strong verb making those six words un-necessary filters).

REDUNDANT: But the longer **we are waiting**, I find myself questioning our decision.
BETTER: But the longer **we wait**, **I find myself questioning** our decision.
BEST: The longer we wait—I question our decision.
(Passive filters to active phrasing).

REDUNDANT: The young lions **are looking** like they'd like to attack.
STILL FILTER DRIVEN: The cubs **look like they'd like to** attack.
BEST: The cubs are poised for attack.
('Are looking' is a passive filter. Young lions can be replaced with one stronger noun. One strong verb—'poised'—replaces 'look like they'd like to').

REDUNDANT: Most of them **will be** crapping their pants **in fear**.
BETTER: Most **of them** will crap their pants.
BEST: Most will crap their pants.
(To 'crap one's pants' is a known term for fear, making 'in fear' a tautology. 'Of them' is an un-necessary filter attached to 'most').

REDUNDANT: The reins **of my** mare.
BETTER: My mare's reins.
('Of my' is rarely needed).

REDUNDANT: I slammed on the brakes **to bring the** car **to a sudden halt**.
BETTER: I slammed on the car's brakes.
('Slammed' makes 'sudden halt' a tautology).

REDUNDANT: I may as well have done the work **myself**.
BETTER: I may as well have done the work.
('I' and 'myself' = tautology).

REDUNDANT: Some **are writhing** in agony on the ground.
BETTER: Some writhe in agony on the ground.
(Change passive filtering to active phrasing).

REDUNDANT: Still, I have to settle the argument.
BETTER: I have to settle the argument.
(Remove filtering and notice how the sentence is strengthened).

REDUNDANT: Now the plan **has been** realised.
BETTER: The plan is realised.
(Change passive filtering to active phrasing).

REDUNDANT: My voice is loud and clear, **with an edge of defiance**.
BETTER: My voice is loud and clear; defiant.
(Change passive filtering to one strong adjective, remove filtering words).

REDUNDANT: I don't turn around but can hear the girls behind me.
BETTER: I can hear the girls behind me.
(Because the girls are behind, and he's relying on the sense of hearing, the reader knows he's looking forwards. The writer doesn't have to spell it out).

REDUNDANT: The adrenalin **is surging** through my body.
BETTER: The adrenalin surges through my body.
(Change passive filtering to active phrasing).

REDUNDANT: I whip my mare around and **she's doing** tight circles.
BETTER: I whip my mare around in tight circles.
(Unnecessary filtering).

REDUNDANT: I see guns **thrown away to the ground** and hands **being** raised.
BETTER: I see guns dropped and hands raised.
('Thrown away to the ground' is replaced by one strong verb. 'Being' is an un-necessary filter because 'I see' implies an action happening).

REDUNDANT: I start yelling.
BETTER: I yell.
(Change passive filtering to active phrasing).

REDUNDANT: There is a feeling of nostalgia **amongst** those **who are** gathered.
BEST: Those gathered are nostalgic.
(Nostalgia is a 'feeling' so there's no need to point it out).

REDUNDANT: I can feel their eyes burning into me.
BETTER: Their eyes burn into me.
(Remove un-necessary filters).

REDUNDANT: I have **been writing** a new short story.
BETTER: I have written a new short story.
(Change passive filtering to active phrasing).

REDUNDANT: Despite **this** though, a thought **still** niggles.
BETTER: Despite this, a thought niggles.
(The word 'niggles' implies a lingering feeling, so 'still' is redundant).

REDUNDANT: For many **it will be** their first taste of seafood.
BETTER: For many it is their first taste of seafood.
(Change passive filtering to active phrasing).

REDUNDANT: They're here because of **a sense of** loyalty.
BETTER: They're here because of loyalty.
(Remove passive filtering).

REDUNDANT: Suddenly I realise that I'd kill for a cup of coffee.
BEST: I'd kill for a cup of coffee.
('Kill' implies an urgent sense, making 'suddenly' redundant. Because the sentence is in first person and begins with I'd, 'I realise' is un-necessary. And *please* use 'suddenly' sparingly—it's a cliché).

REDUNDANT: My mind **is racing**.
BETTER: My mind races.
(Change passive filtering to active phrasing).

REDUNDANT: 'It must be done.' **And in the end, hers were the final words on the matter.**
BETTER: 'It must be done.' Hers were the final words.
BEST: 'It must be done.'
(If 'It must be done' is the final sentence in a short story – 'hers were the final words' becomes redundant. Physically having those as the final words on the page is powerful).

REDUNDANT: Laurie smiled as she gazed **back** at Steve.
BETTER: Laurie smiled as she gazed at Steve.
(If the character is doing one thing, and then does another, back is understood).

REDUNDANT: Mel **continued** to stare at the mess in front of her.
BETTER: Mel stared at the mess in front of her.
(If a character hasn't stopped doing an action, there is no need to state they continued doing something).

REDUNDANT: Sawyer **began** to giggle.
BETTER: Sawyer giggled.

REDUNDANT: He went to sit and landed on the floor **instead**.
BETTER: He went to sit and landed on the floor.
(What didn't happen is usually made obvious because you have stated what did happen).

REDUNDANT: I drove them **both** to the police station.
BETTER: I drove them to the police station.
('Them' signposts plural, therefore 'both' is unnecessary).

REDUNDANT: I walked **down** to the local bakery.
BETTER: I walked to the local bakery.
(Signposts like 'up' and 'down' and 'along' are rarely needed. The reader gets it).

REDUNDANT & PASSIVE: I **had come up** to Queensland from Tasmania.
BETTER: I came to Queensland from Tasmania.
(Avoid passive phrasing like 'had come', and directional stage instructions like 'up').

REDUNDANT: Dylan **went and** collected Bryce from school.
BETTER: Dylan collected Bryce from school.

REDUNDANT: She liked to play the game **called** 'Guess Who'.
BETTER: She liked to play **the game** 'Guess Who'.
BEST: She liked to play 'Guess Who'.
(The use of the word 'play' signposts that it is a game, making 'game' redundant).

REDUNDANT: **Many of** the soccer players were out of uniform.
BETTER: The soccer players were out of uniform.
('Of' in general is a weak word that should be eliminated. Especially 'off of').

REDUNDANT: Notice how the entry is short—874 words when 1,000 **words** were allowed.
BETTER: Notice how the entry is short—874 words when 1,000 were allowed.
(Avoid repetition; readers only need to be told once).

REDUNDANT: Stephanie considered his reply, and **then** smiled.
BETTER: Stephanie considered his reply and smiled.
(If an action follows, *then* is implied).

REDUNDANT: The door **to the** office was locked.
BETTER: The office door was locked.
(Using the phrase 'to the' often causes wordiness).

Examples of often used redundant filter words include:

considered	regarded	wondered	saw
heard	hoped	realised	smelled
watched	touched	felt	knew
decided	just	really	to be
reaching	suddenly	that	you know
up	down	in	out
anyway	even	quite	rather
very	almost	back	continued
began	started	had	smiled

There are more, many more.

Tell instead of show, and the over-use of filters and adverbs are the biggest issues I see separating mediocre short stories from the exceptional.

The practice of self-editing tautologies and filters from prose, improves future draft writing. However, don't be overly critical of yourself. A professional writer of over thirty years, my first draft writing still contains tautologies and filters because our inner thoughts and natural dialogue are jam-packed with them.

With experience, common tautologies and filters will disappear naturally from your draft writing allowing self-editing to focus on more complex examples.

The holy grail of writing is to place the reader inside the action.

FILTER DRIVEN FIRST DRAFT: My dog could barely lift his head. It seemed to me that that the vet was uncaring. He most likely did this ten times a week, but for me, I was losing my best friend. A tear slid down my cheek as I thought of all the good times we had together over 18 years.

FILTER-FREE, READER IN ACTION: Happy lifted his head, but it fell. Smack. Eyes soulful, weary. I held his gaze. Stroked his fur. Pain, trust, love mirrored from his sorrowful, glazed eyes. My breathing sped to match his panting … in out, in out, in out. Saliva dropped. I gently wiped his snout. He closed his eyes … once … twice. His chest stilled. My ugly snaffle and rolling tears hastened the vet to close the door and leave me alone with my best friend.

In the final pages of this book are exercises to practise your growing knowledge base to write active, filter free prose that places your reader inside the action.

CHAPTER SIX

ENTER LATE, LEAVE EARLY

By C. Sawyer

I drum into writers—follow the competition guidelines, and don't go over competition word counts! Writers *might* be forgiven a 10% discrepancy, but never more, and why give judges a reason to discount a story that took much effort to write? In a strong field, it's an easy first cull to discount entries that don't adhere to competition guidelines.

And I'll give a tip, to many editors and competition judges it appears amateurish when writers submit right on the word limit—being under the word limit showcases professionalism and efficiency.

If I had an Astin Martin for every time a writer said, 'But I'll lose the essence of my story if I delete any more!' my whole suburb could be James Bond wannabes.

Writers often underestimate the intelligence of their audience. The dreaded background information dump at the start of a story kills the oomph of the launch and wreaks havoc on word count. And over-explaining an ending kills it just as dead.

My advice for accomplished writers: *Enter your story as late as possible and leave your story as early as possible.* To:

1. Avoid the writers' foible of laboured exposition at the commencement of the story.
2. Throw the reader straight into the thick of the action—where the story is interesting.
3. Leave the reader at the point of a-ha—not later.

Writers sometimes think their reader needs to know everything that's in the writer's head to understand their character. They don't.

Readers intuit meaning from subtle nuances. It is this exercising of a reader's mind that marries them to a story. They're on the journey with the characters.

Consider this background info dump beginning:

> Mr Colonel, that's what the students called him. Or if they played on the basketball team, the kids were more familiar, 'Hey Colonel' being the norm. He was 68 years old and tired. He'd been employed at Redcliffe State High School for forty years. He'd never made it to the rank of Principal. Truth be told, he wasn't that good with adults. The thought of managing 40 year-old women through menopause and

raising kids ... jeez he'd rather hoik himself from his boat into shark infested waters. So he'd stayed the manual arts teacher. It was about time he retired though, he thought to himself on this day, Monday 13th June, as he walked into the school grounds. Coaching basketball kept him from being a cranky old man, but his legs were so rickety now that he could no longer run the length of the court. He would hand in his resignation next week. He'd be just in time to train for the Nationals with his bowls team. They needed him. Without him, there's no way they'd make the finals.

That was the last conscious thought Clive Colonel had on this earth. The knife sheared him from behind, straight through his kidney. He dropped like a sack of potatoes. The spreading pool of blood had no witness—students fled as the maniacal eyes of Jason Fletcher searched for his next victim. (231 words).

That's the writer getting their character down on paper and showing off about what a wonderful creator of characters they are. Later the reader will learn that Jason didn't make the basketball team. The story is about Jason Fletcher and why he murdered his basketball coach and members of the celebrated team, so the writer should get there as quickly as possible—and launch with the action to grab their audience.

Consider this trimmed version that whacks the reader in the guts:

> Monday 13th June and Redcliffe State High School; those two details would be forever linked to basketball coach, Colonel. The teacher had no way of knowing this as his rickety legs carried him into school for what he'd announced would be the second last week of a 40-year career.
>
> The knife sheared him from behind, straight through his kidney. He dropped like a sack of potatoes. The spreading pool of blood had no witness—students fled as the maniacal eyes of Jason Fletcher searched for his next victim. (88 words).

Now, here's the writer explaining the ending:

> So in the end it had nothing to do with basketball after all. Everyone always speculated why Coach Colonel never married. Some thought him a cad—simply too charming to settle for just one woman. But in the absence of evidence, others wondered if he were gay, and since he was from the time when homosexuality was not brought into the open, he just never came out. No one guessed the truth. The love of his life died in childbirth and knowing he couldn't look at the child without blaming him for her death, he gave the child up for adoption.
>
> And that child, as it became known on this fateful day, was Jason Fletcher. Molested in childhood, brainwashed by the loose lips of a

well-meaning but misguided aunt. The fruit doesn't fall far from the tree. For as Colonel couldn't forgive the son, the son couldn't forgive him. (148 words)

The above ending is over explained. A better ending would *leave early*:

> Senior Detective Newman looked at the broken man. They'd been in this room for 26 hours. He reclaimed his seat. 'Jason, we've just had a visit from Family Services.'
> Jason showed no reaction.
> 'I know you're adopted, and I know your adoptive father molested you.'
> Jason's upper lip spasmed into a snarl, and he glared at the detective.
> 'We've also been through your phone. We know you talked to Marjorie Jackson, maiden name Colonel.'
> Jason's head dipped, black eyes looked straight ahead.
> 'She told us what she told you.'
> 'And what was that?' snarled Jason.
> 'That her brother knew he couldn't keep you, that he knew he'd always blame you.'
> 'Fruit doesn't fall far from the tree hey.' With those words Jason's bravado evaporated. His head fell into his hands, body wracked by pain. (134 words).

At this point the reader experiences the thrill of connecting the dots. A-ha. Satisfaction. The end.

Enter late, leave early is a tertiary skill that signifies a seasoned writer; as is compelling dialogue, the subject of the next chapter.

CHAPTER SEVEN

BFFS: HOW DIALOGUE MAKES PLOT, THEME & CONFLICT SHINE

By L. E. Daniels

IN simplest terms, fiction is conflict. In short fiction, one clear conflict is the undercurrent that propels the plot, even in the moments of dialogue. Key moments of dialogue can serve as 'best friends forever' for plot, theme and conflict, making them sparkle and shine. When its potential is tapped, dialogue enhances cohesion and advances the narrative—steady as a BFF who's always got time to talk.

Writers hit high notes when they use dialogue to do *at least* these three things:

- drive the plot,
- reflect the theme, and

- underscore the conflict.

Dialogue offers a multitude of other effects like characterisation, setting, humour and other emotional textures, etc., but it should at least incorporate these three prominent strategies.

Short stories don't have a lot of elbow room, so it's crucial to use literary tools with precision—dialogue especially—and sometimes we need to adjust the way we see a tool in order to use it more effectively. Instead of looking at dialogue as a way to share information about the world, backstory, and character motivations, we can see dialogue as yet another dimension of the story itself.

First, writers must read. As Stephen King typed in a letter to me in 1988, 'READ READ READ' and he meant it. As we read, we note the writer's techniques and approaches.

Study the dialogue of Anton Chekhov. As Titian is the painter's painter, Chekhov is the writer's writer. He can teach us so much about the craft, when we simply take the time to observe. For Chekhov, dialogue always deepens the conflict and the plot, even in his shortest stories. Often, he uses dialogue to disguise a character's thoughts and motivations. His characters show us who they are by what they say *and* what they withhold. He emphasises the point clearly in his work: **Dialogue isn't just about what's said. It's also about what isn't said at all.**

Next is my handy list of how to get the most out of each moment of dialogue.

Cut adverbs within dialogue by 90%.

We're taught to use adverbs in primary school but they are actually the bloated leeches of good prose that tell more than show

... so step on them. Stephen King wrote '...the road to hell is paved with adverbs' in *On Writing*. Think about it: *speaking awkwardly* is not as awkward as showing characters use um and ah and fidget through their lines. I have seen 'he said laughingly' enough times to make me weep. Just cut most of them right out.

Use plain verbs like said/asked/shouted/cried but refrain from most of the ridiculous and complex dialogue attribution verbs seen in badly written primary school readers.

You know them by heart. Rebuked. Declared. Consoled. Chided. Yes, we learned to read with these but they don't belong in polished, professional prose. I despise them because they're showy and distracting when they are supposed to be invisible. We want readers to hear the dialogue in their minds, not stumble through a minefield of clunky verbs. Who chortles? No one.

Write dialogue so each character's voice sounds so unique, it can almost be read without any dialogue attribution at all.

That's a great discipline and fulfilling writing goal. Readers will know intuitively who is speaking by the language chosen by the characters and the healthy amount of characterisation instilled in their lines. We write, overwrite, revise, cut and rewrite until the characters sound like themselves.

Avoid those dreaded info dumps.

Sometimes writers use dialogue as a way to convey information. This works if it's subtle, but if the dialogue comes off like, 'Hello, let me tell you about the twenty years of war, son, that has ravaged our countryside… something you would know already because you live here…' or 'Hello, stranger, let me describe to you how all this technology works in the year 3000…' the illusion of story is broken, the pace falters and the readers wake from the dream of story. Readers are instantly reminded that they are in fact, just reading, and not experiencing the dialogue in their minds.

Observe the patterns and lengths of dialogue in a story.

Read the short story aloud to hear how long the conversations ensue and how long readers have to wait for the next moment of action. More often than not, dialogue is overwritten in our early drafts and needs refining. Sometimes, they're too short and need to bring something more to the table before the moment ends. Either way, we can ask ourselves: Does this conversation drive the plot? Reflect the theme? Underscore the conflict? These questions can help us extend or truncate our dialogue drafts for precision.

Cut the chit-chat and banter pretending to be dialogue.

This is a big one. Early drafts may contain moments of dialogue that ramble or just kind of 'happen', but don't really drive the narrative forward. They can be a way for us writers to get to know our characters, but they don't need to stay. If they don't deliver on plot, conflict or theme, revise them. The best moments of dialogue shine as bright as a plot point or a beat of dramatic action. They read as essential to the storyline and we can tell because if they are cut, the story suffers.

Consider what's left unsaid as much as what's said.

Chekhov's stories are free online so you can read them before bed and stew in them as you sleep. He reminds us that in real life, people rarely spell out what they really think and feel. People can be purposely misleading, deeply guarded, and even uncertain of what they truly think and feel. Also remember that dialogue in a story is not a transcription of real conversation. People do tend to go on a bit and repeat themselves in real life and we don't need to read that on the page. When we're serving something for the eyes and the mind, it has to be different from what we serve to the ears. *It has to be more precise.*

Check for repetitive patterns in dialogue.

Read through all the moments of dialogue in your draft and hunt for unconscious patterns. Are there lots of repeated words or characterisation devices? Does one character end way too many sentences with 'bro' and does another smile again and again? If you're writing about women, apply the Bechdel-Wallace test. Ensure the female characters discuss topics other than males across the dialogues of your story.

Punctuate dialogue correctly and use any quality piece of published fiction as a guide.

Editors and literary judges despair the number of manuscripts they see with mispunctuated dialogue. Handing over messy dialogue to an editor is like asking them to clean your room for you. Please don't. Writers want to master punctuation to ensure that we convey the meaning, pauses, tone and textures we have in mind.

For some dialogue analysis, see the excerpt below from Anton Chekhov's famous story, 'The Kiss'. Yes, it blows off the advice on adverbs and even the word 'very', but it's a story from another time and still, the usage of both are not intrusive.

The end advice is this: like all artists, writers weigh everything and use these tools with clear intent.

'A strange thing happened to me at those Von Rabbeks',' he began, trying to put an indifferent and ironical tone into his voice. 'You know I went into the billiard-room …'

He began describing very minutely the incident of the kiss, and a moment later relapsed into silence… In the course of that moment he had told everything, and it surprised him dreadfully to find how short a time it took him to tell it. He had imagined that he could have been telling the story of the kiss till next morning. Listening to him, Lobytko, who was a great liar and consequently believed no one, looked at him sceptically and laughed. Merzlyakov twitched his eyebrows and, without removing his eyes from *The Messenger of Europe* said:

'That's an odd thing! How strange! ... throws herself on a man's neck, without addressing him by name... She must be some sort of hysterical neurotic.'

'Yes, she must,' Ryabovitch agreed.

'A similar thing once happened to me,' said Lobytko, assuming a scared expression. 'I was going last year to Kovno... I took a second-class ticket. The train was crammed, and it was impossible to sleep. I gave the guard half a rouble; he took my luggage and led me to another compartment... I lay down and covered myself with a rug... It was dark, you understand. Suddenly I felt someone touch me on the shoulder and breathe in my face. I made a movement with my hand and felt somebody's elbow... I opened my eyes and only imagine—a woman. Black eyes, lips red as a prime salmon, nostrils breathing passionately—a bosom like a buffer...'

'Excuse me,' Merzlyakov interrupted calmly, 'I understand about the bosom, but how could you see the lips if it was dark?'

Remember, quality dialogue:

- Has minimal adverbs.
- Uses plain speech tags like said/asked/shouted/cried.
- Has nuanced patterns attributed to each character.
- Does not contain information dumps.
- Is not over-written.
- Is used to drive the plot, reflect the theme, or underscore the conflict.

- Is essential to the story.
- Plays on what's not said, as well as what is.
- Does not contain overly repetitive patterns.
- Is punctuated correctly.

CHAPTER EIGHT

POV: WHO'S THE BOSS?

By L. E. Daniels

POINT of view (POV), also called perspective, is all about who's the boss of the story. One of the more technical aspects of fiction, it takes practise to master. The best stories have integrity in the POV, meaning that once they establish perspective, it's consistent.

One question comes up a lot in workshops: 'But isn't whether a story is good just subjective? Isn't it just a matter of opinion anyway?'

No. Not at all.

When used with skill, literary devices captivate our readers without their knowing it. When we're sloppy, we lose them just as fast and wake them from the dream of our stories. Just like how visitors might not notice if our home is tidy, they notice if it's not.

If readers are unaware of POV, or if more skilled readers appreciate how a story entrances them—it's working.

Yes, point of view is challenging. I don't recall anyone teaching me POV in depth. My professors just used the terminology and expected me to grasp it. Looking back, I think no one taught it in depth because POV is difficult to describe coherently. It takes a meticulous approach to do it well.

Editing other writers' work and honing my own writing showed me what it looks like when POV goes wrong, and when it goes right—for emerging and established writers alike. It's good to remember that even the author of several published books might have slips in POV in a draft and still needs an editor to tag them.

So let's walk through this slowly. Take a break from this chapter if it gets slippery and come back to it later. Look at your favourite stories, too, and trace the way POV is used. Reading and tracing POV like a writer—a keen observer—helps us tremendously.

While a novel might systematically offer multiple points of view from several characters (see *The Poisonwood Bible* by Barbara Kingsolver, or *Mudbound* by Hillary Jordan as examples) or shift between 3rd person limited and 3rd person omniscient (see *Where the Crawdads Sing* by Delia Owens), a short story has less time for variation. The rules for short stories are strict, otherwise we end up with something called head-hopping and it confuses the reader and looks something like this:

> Rex fed kindling into the fire, one twig at a time until the glow warmed his face and he knew everything would be all right. He sat back on a log, relief spreading like the heat, and poked at the growing flames with a stick. *(Here, we experience 3rd person POV limited to Rex, we witness*

action close to him and feel his relief.) Cooper squatted by the fire, adding a handful of dry gum leaves, pleased with the heat. *(First wobble here. Rex should see/hear Cooper before the reader does. Readers need to see that Cooper is pleased through Rex's senses.)*

'Nice,' he told Rex. He thought the rain would never let up enough for a fire. *(Another wobble as we read Cooper's thoughts.)*

Rex slid a cooking rack over the fire, signalling to Cooper to stop adding leaves to his fire. *(In simplest terms, the inner thoughts of two characters cannot be written in the same section—that is head-hopping).*

Here it is remedied for clarity:

Rex fed kindling into the fire, one twig at a time until the glow warmed his face and he knew everything would be all right. He sat back on a log, relief spreading like the heat, and poked at the growing flames with a stick.

Cooper's boots crackled across the leaf litter as he approached and squatted by the fire. He added a handful of dry gum leaves and Rex caught their oily scent in the rising smoke.

'Nice,' Cooper said. 'I thought the rain would never let up enough for a fire.'

Rex slid a cooking rack over the fire, signalling to Cooper to stop adding leaves to his fire.

Head-hopping between characters within one scene confuses readers. The audience takes cues from the author from the opening lines regarding who to follow, who to trust, and how to perceive the action. POV is truly the axis, or the boss, of a story.

Let's break POV into sections, step through its different forms, and the advantages and disadvantages of each. We've also supplied a writing prompt with each section to encourage experimentation.

1st Person POV: Told from the 'I' perspective, the protagonist is also the narrator. In a short story, this can mean the narrator has lived to tell the tale and can signal the ending or consequences to the reader, unless the speaker is a ghost or the story is told in the present tense. First person tells readers immediately who is driving the story.

ADVANTAGE: Intimate narration, the reader is privy to the speaker's thoughts and secrets. Action reads as immediate, even if the story is recounted in past tense.
DISADVANTAGE: Readers only access what is in the narrator's tight field of vision and experience. Stories don't usually shift from 1st to other perspectives, so 1st remains the POV for the whole story.
STORY POTENTIAL: Handy for unreliable narration, where the reader slowly discovers the speaker is dishonest or manipulative.

EXAMPLE:

> On my knees in the garden, I tore out weeds until my hands cracked. I should have worn gloves. My body pushed through thick ginger stalks and leggy dracaena and

spiders dropped on my head, but I refused to return to the house; not until the rage passed through my chest and down my arms and surrendered into the cool brown earth.

Try This: Remember when you were angry and took some time to think in order to get a handle on this fierce emotion. Place a character into those feelings and let them tell the story for you, from the 'I'.

Styles of 1ˢᵗ Person POV

Interior Monologue: The reader tunes directly into stream of consciousness, as if hearing thoughts of the protagonist as they unfold.

> Oh my God, please let him be all right. I'll do anything if you'll just let him be all right. I am so sorry that I slept late and missed the alarm and then sped all the way to the station. I can't believe I hit him …

Dramatic Monologue: The reader overhears someone speaking aloud to another person.

> Eleven o'clock. A knock at the door … I hope I haven't disturbed you, madam. You weren't asleep—were you? But I've just given my lady her tea, and there was such a nice cup …
>
> *The Lady's Maid* by Katherine Mansfield.

Letter Narration: Reader experiences written monologue, usually a letter, email, or text these days.

> Miss Margaret Cresswell, Matron, House of Industry, Toronto—To Mr. Simon Herron, North Hudson, January 15, 1852.
>
> Since your letter is accompanied by an endorsement by your minister, I am happy to reply … We do not have any girl at the Home who is of marriageable age, since we send our girls out to make a living usually around the age of fourteen or fifteen, but we do keep track of them for some years or usually until they are married.
>
> *A Wilderness Station* by Alice Munro.

Diary/Journal Narration: Diarists recount events and stop-start as they unfold in entries; the action reads as quite immediate and serialised.

> It is very seldom that mere ordinary people like John and myself secure ancestral halls for the summer. A colonial mansion, a hereditary estate, I would say a haunted house, and reach the height of romantic felicity—but that would be asking too much of fate!
>
> *The Yellow Wallpaper* by Charlotte Gilman.

Subjective Narration: Reader is told by one of the characters after the events of the story concluded.

I know what is being said about me and you can take my side or theirs, that's your own business. It's my word against Eunice's and Olivia Ann's, and it should be plain enough to anyone with two good eyes which one of us has their wits about them.
My Side of the Matter by Truman Capote.

Detached Autobiography: A reliable narrator guides the reader through each scene of the story, which reads as a kind of believable or 'true story' on behalf of the author.

All the trouble began when my grandfather died and my grandmother—my father's mother—came to live with us. Relations in the one house are a strain at the best of times, but, to make matters worse, my grandmother was a real old countrywoman and quite unsuited to the life in town. She had a fat, wrinkled old face, and, to Mother's great indignation, went round the house in bare feet—the boots had her crippled, she said.
First Confession by Frank O'Connor.

2nd Person POV: Makes 'you' the protagonist and is a semi-aggressive form that pulls readers into the story by the lapels. A point of view that makes a strong point, it can be seen in long form in the novel *Bright Lights, Big City* by Jay McInerney as an effective way to convey a sense of drug addiction.

ADVANTAGE: Powerful prose and high energy. Great for social, cultural or political statements.
DISADVANTAGE: It can read as overly prescriptive, didactic or just plain exhausting.
STORY POTENTIAL: Makes great flash fiction (stories usually a couple to a few hundred words, and under 1000).

> Hang the clothes before 7am and bring them in before 4pm, or they'll stink. Make the lunches just right—remember their favourites and don't pack too much or too little. Tell the kids to brush their teeth and forget to brush your own. Drive the kids to school and smile at the other mothers with your mouth closed. Rush home and turn on the computer while brushing your teeth. Spill your coffee on your shirt and leave it because you have a deadline. Watch the sky through your window while you work. If it rains, you'll have to wash those clothes again.

Try this: Consider an aspect of life, an emotion, or a process you know intimately. Write a few lines in the 2nd person POV.

3rd Person POV Limited: The most common POV found in contemporary short fiction, it is told from the perspective of he, she, it, they. Imagine a camera following the protagonist closely throughout the story. As in the example below, we only ever get to experience the internal thoughts and feelings of that character. As an editor, I've seen the most head-hopping overtake this particular POV.

ADVANTAGE: The protagonist tells the story from centre stage. Everything is witnessed from that character's POV, as if a camera is perched close by but not inside the speaker. Has a stronger sense of objectivity than 1st person POV because the narrator is not the same identity as the protagonist.

DISADVANTAGE: All thoughts or feelings of others must be perceived by the protagonist. The protagonist must always be in the room, with no scenes unfolding without him or her.

STORY POTENTIAL: A tight, close narrative with a powerful lead.

> The grandmother did not want to go to Florida. She wanted to visit some of her connections in east Tennessee and she was seizing at every chance to change Bailey's mind. Bailey was the son she lived with, her only boy. He was sitting on the edge of the chair at the table, bent over the orange sports section of the *Journal*. 'Now look here, Bailey,' she said, 'see here, read this,' and she stood with one hand on her thin hip and the other rattling the newspaper at his bald head. 'Here this fellow that calls himself The Misfit is aloose from the Federal Pen and headed toward Florida and you read here what it says he did to these people. Just you read it. I wouldn't take my children in any direction with a criminal like that aloose in it. I couldn't answer to my conscience if I did.'
>
> *A Good Man is Hard to Find*, Flannery O'Connor.

3rd Person POV Dual: Traditional narration expands to glimpse inner life of two particular characters signalling a particular purpose. Here are two sections from two different points of view.

Esme's baby was sick. His little brown body hung across her lap, damp with fever. He hardly moved. Watching the rapid rise and fall of his little chest, Esme knew she had to get them to listen. She had to try again.
…

He recoiled from the woman and her infant. These people landed here day and night; sick, even drunk, all looking for a free pass. He never got a free pass. The woman pleaded with him in broken English and reached for him but he pulled away from her. He was determined to get his lunch before calling the doctor again.

3rd Person POV Multiple: Usually found in novels rather than short stories, there are examples which include three or more character points of view to convey the narrative. Examples include:

'Fever Flower' by Shirley Ann Grau.
'The Suicides of Private Greaves' by James Moffet.
'Inez' by Merle Hodge.

Note: Double line breaks within the story indicate both a scene break and a POV shift.

For 3rd Person POV Dual and Multiple
ADVANTAGE: A breadth of a confronting issue or theme can be explored with multiple, even contradicting points of view.
DISADVANTAGE: The writer has to work hard to give each POV equal time and ensure the reader always knows who is the centre of each scene.

STORY POTENTIAL: Inspiring compassion or a deeper understanding of a complex issue like racism, historical bias, or the human condition.

3rd Person POV Omniscient or Objective: The rarest POV found in contemporary short stories, the narrator is either 1.) omniscient and godlike or 2.) reporting from objective, hidden-camera like viewpoint.

For the omniscient perspective, the narrator might tap into some of the characters' inner thoughts and feelings, but in a balanced and nonjudgmental way.

For the objective perspective, the narrator reports events as they occur as if broadcast from what a camera could record, allowing readers more room to interpret them. There may be some observation of the characters' thoughts and feelings, but only as observable, external details like a smile or a shrug.

The narrator in the following example reads in 3rd person POV omniscient. Note how the narrator hovers above the action and conveys the state of mind of everyone in turn.

> The dogs barking at the edge of the property rattled everyone at the kitchen table. Father stood and disappeared for a moment to get his rifle from the locker. Mother went straight for the phone and called the police. The children whimpered and sat motionless except for their eyes.

The narrator in the Hemingway story below is in 3rd person POV objective, merely reporting what he sees occurring between these two characters:

> The American and the girl with him sat at a table in the shade, outside the building. It was very hot and the express from Barcelona would come in forty minutes. It stopped at this junction for two minutes and went to Madrid.
>
> *The Hills Like White Elephants*, Ernest Hemingway.

Try This: Imagine a setting that makes you uncomfortable. Stage two people within it who have just had a heated argument, e.g., a busy restaurant, a parade ground, Christmas shopping at the mall, maybe even a crusader playing chess with Death. Write a few lines as a non-judgemental observer from this POV.

For 3rd Person POV Omniscient or Objective
ADVANTAGE: Suspension of all judgement.
DISADVANTAGE: Heavily controlled or an outright lack of intimacy with characters can leave readers a bit cold.
STORY POTENTIAL: Taboo subjects can be explored at a distance.

All of this is a lot to absorb. Give it time. Have a look at the creative writing exercises at the back of the book to hone your skills.

Experimenting by rewriting the same text from various POV is an excellent exercise to sharpen writing skills and reveal opportunities within a short story. Practise also assists in identifying any head-hopping in a text, which brings us to our next chapter—The Art of Self Editing.

CHAPTER NINE

THE ART OF SELF-EDITING

By C. Sawyer & L. E. Daniels

EDITING is a crucial step in the path to publication. It ensures that we mean what we say and say what we mean: the story and messages we hope to convey are the ones our readers receive.

When we write the first draft, we're writing for ourselves. When we're editing, we're the reader's advocate.

No writer's first draft is a masterpiece. Our short story will always be better after we've read it aloud and considered how each word in every sentence contributes to its rhythm and intent. In this chapter, we look at the knowledge a writer possesses, with more emphasis on topics not covered in preceding chapters, to conduct a successful self-edit.

Labeled 'a literary genius', Elmore Leonard famously said, 'When you write, try to leave out the parts that readers tend to skip.' Simple … yes. Complex to learn. There's much throat clearing for writers to work through to get there.

Associate Professor Roslyn Petelin, author of *How Writing Works* said, 'We write our first draft so that we have something to revise.'

Earnest Hemingway, succinct as ever, shared his wisdom on the matter: 'The first draft of anything is shit.'

Editing flenses the story down to its necessary bones, cutting away the digressions and subplots that don't add to the narrative. It shapes the story into a pleasurable reading experience, fleshing out the plot's skeleton with scenes and sensations that pull the reader deep into the story world. Tight writing doesn't necessarily mean fewer words; it means the words on the page earn their place.

Self-editing is much more than checking spelling and grammar. It's our chance to consider:

- Does the beginning GRAB?
- Have I killed the ending with too much description?
- Do my characters have realistic flaws?
- Does my dialogue sound genuine?
- Do my characters speak differently from each other, or do they all just sound like me?
- Do I need to fix information dumps?
- Can I replace two words with one strong one?
- Have I used shorter sentences at moments of high tension?
- Can I delete any filters and tautologies, and re-word passive phrasing?

- Is the work structured and signposted for the audience?
- Are there sequencing or timing issues?
- Have I maintained a single point of view (POV) per scene?
- Have I avoided clichés and adverbs?
- Have I avoided the urge to explain?

The term 'revise' derives from the Latin 'to see back' so it literally means 're-see'. Revision lets us step back from the work and consider if the words on the page best convey the story in our imaginations. The key to successful revision is to consider one aspect of the work at a time. Or as Associate Professor Petelin says, 'You loop through your document several times, examining a different feature each time, remembering that good writing is as much a matter of subtraction as of creation.'

At the end of this chapter, we've included a self-editing checklist. Complete one task per read-through as you loop through your revisions. For now, let's take a closer look at the essential steps of a seriously good self-edit.

Highlight Story Structure

- Map the moments of rising action, the change that occurs in the main character, the climax, and the resolution.
- Does the beginning hook the reader and has the story commenced at an action point? Or does the story commence with throat clearing (i.e., the author writing their way into the story with unnecessary details such as scenes of the character waking up)? Are there enough

moments of rising action (ideally three, with each moment more significant than the last)?
- Are there shorter sentences at moments of high tension? Read the story aloud to consider the pace for each sentence.
- Has the ending been killed with too much detail? Keep in mind—enter late, leave early.

Highlight Adverb/Verb Combinations

Mark all the adverb/verb combinations in the story, e.g., tiptoed very quietly or spoke loudly. Replace those highlighted with strong verbs. In the examples above, 'tiptoed' stands alone. Very quietly is unnecessary because tiptoed means very quietly. In the second example, 'spoke loudly' should be replaced by a strong verb like 'roared'.

Regarding 'very', Mark Twain wrote: 'Substitute "damn" every time you're inclined to write "very"; your editor will delete it and the writing will be just as it should be.' Good advice.

Example, poor: Kitty spoke loudly and all eyes in the classroom swung quickly towards her.

Example, good: Kitty roared and all eyes in the classroom darted her way.

Example, poor: Aiden tiptoed very quietly and carefully stuck his head through the open doorway. He jumped back hurriedly when he saw the teacher writing carefully on the blackboard.

Example, good: Aiden tiptoed to the doorway and peeked. Seeing the teacher labouring over words on the blackboard, he recoiled.

The more we practise this editing process, the better we get at choosing strong verbs in writing. Strong verbs draw vivid worlds in our story.

Highlight Tautologies & Filters

Use of filtering words is the most common problem writers have in first-draft writing, and a culprit contributing to writing being over word counts. Filters and tautologies are redundant words, and place distance between the story and the reader. See chapter Let's Talk Tautologies & Filters for examples.

Redundant words are better in dialogue because they reflect how real people speak, but even there should be used just enough to make an impression and not overdrawn.

Highlight Info Dumps

Big chunks of telling that reveal backstory, setting, character motivation, etc., make the reader's eyes glaze because the story grinds to a halt for exposition.

Consider any passage where you've placed a block of background information, and where possible, rewrite that information by scattering it throughout your characters' actions and dialogue. The reader doesn't need to know everything about the lead character at the beginning of the story. Sprinkle details throughout the story for an enjoyable unravelling for the reader.

Avoid dumping large blocks of background information in a character's dialogue, e.g.,

> Last year when I drove the Volkswagen car that Dad and I rebuilt along John Street—the street I grew up in from 1991 – 2010—I saw you walking on the footpath past the haunted house and I wondered at the time how often you thought of me and all the times we played spin the bottle in there with the whole crew from school: Cherie, Lisa, Sharron, Tyler, Brad and Vinnie.

Real people don't talk like this, but you'd be surprised how many writers try to sneak inauthentic sentences of dialogue into their writing.

A better way to write the above, and considering that the rebuilt car, the time period, and the names of the crew from school are essential to the story arc, would be:

> John's cheeks warmed but he was way too suave at 30 to let his feelings escalate to a crimson shade. His high school crush. Oh, the nights of spin the bottle in the old haunted house… 'You haven't changed a bit.'
>
> 'You have,' she replied. 'There's something about you.' Her head tilted. Green eyes mirrored their history, then shock when she saw the scar.
>
> 'Last year.' His hand rubbed the line that ran from his ear and disappeared inside his shirt.
>
> 'How?'
>
> 'Crash. Remember the VW?'

'Of course. You and your Dad spent hours rebuilding that bloody thing, it was so boring.'

John's laugh was genuine. She'd always excited him. She was forthright, not afflicted by the need to be liked. 'Remember John Street?'

'So, you mean, what went on in the haunted house?'

'Well, yeah.' Their eyes held, smoldering. 'You heard I'm a detective now?'

'Yep.'

'I was following a suspect along John Street last year, got rammed at a cross section by another car.'

'Damn, that's unlucky.'

'Not luck; they targeted me.'

Her eyes blinked, a veil descended. She took a half step back and John saw the flirty sway in her hip disappear, back straighten.

'I saw you just beforehand, near the haunted house.'

'That was you?'

He nodded.

'Didn't realise.'

'Anyway, I was wondering, have you seen any of the old crew? Tyler, Brad, Vinnie … I lost touch with them once I was in the force.'

She looked at him, considering. 'Sharron and Lisa, I see them from time to time. Cherie—not so much. She stuck with the boys. The rest of us moved on.'

'I see.'

'I'm not so sure you do,' she replied. 'Look, I've gotta go.'

He grabbed her arm to stop her. 'They did this to me.'

Regret, resignation. He was surprised he didn't see fear.

'I can't help you.'

He watched her leave.

Highlight Dialogue

Essentially, we should be able to strip away speech tags, read the dialogue aloud, and the audience will know which characters say what. We get this result if we've crafted nuanced speech patterns and used dialogue as a way to showcase the personality, motivation and the temperament of each character.

Remember that nobody speaks in continuous, fully formed, long sentences. Real people speak in half sentences, half thoughts; often speaking before they think, and rarely saying what they really mean.

Consider the silences and what's not said. Sometimes our characters can reply to another's body language—a vastly rewarding level of stage directions ready to deliver for our scenes. See chapter on BFFs: How Dialogue Makes Plot, Theme & Conflict Shine to refresh the minutiae.

Highlight Show Not Tell

Seeing is believing, whereas people only listen to a small portion of what we tell them. The same works for writing. Review chapter Hint, Tantalise, Reel Me In for more insight, but let's review for the sake of our editing approach.

Showing gives readers evidence and allows them to come to their own understanding. Scenes and dramatic action trust the reader to piece together what is happening and why, and this is why readers read. Readers want to intuit, rather than be told, a character's motivation. They want to distil an emotional state. They want to come to the conclusion that the factory being closed is the reason the family has nothing to eat. Readers want to be detectives in a sense, and uncover what's driving the story, and writers need to remember that. When we read vivid description, the parts of our brains that fire up with the same stimuli in real life are triggered. That's the red hot centre of a writer's power.

Telling gives the reader the conclusion, labels the emotions, intellectualises the potential for tension, and creates narrative distance. While telling can be useful to transition between scenes and to summarise action that has happened before, brevity works best. Telling can move things along but can bypass the opportunity to give the reader an immersive experience. Too much telling flattens a piece into a kind of speech.

For an example of how telling can work, imagine a colourful description of a man gazing from the window of a rotten old house, at a blackening sea. See the dark clouds cloaking the sunset and the empty, stony beach lined with beach grass and thorny brambles. Let the prose light upon a lonely fishing trawler chugging towards the decrepit marina and a solitary seagull preening on a post. Then end the paragraph with lines like, *No moon rises over this haunted place. He is all alone and terrified.*

That's showing punctuated by a blow of telling in the right spot, to accentuate and sharpen a mood, but it does not rely upon telling to drive the story.

It's important to highlight that most of our first drafts are telling and that we often need to tell our stories first in order to show them. Once we've gotten that first draft out of our heads and onto the page, however, we can mark passages of telling, and ask 'How is this moment acted out?'

Lastly and through self-editing, we can pepper our scenes with moments of telling that land a crisp message on the page in just the right spots for maximum impact.

Highlight Cliché

One of the first things many professors do in Creative Writing 101 is ask students to write a story then return it with all the clichés circled with the note: *Rewrite in your own words.*

We all slip into clichés in our first drafts. Like telling the story before showing it, defaulting to info dumps, or bashing out crummy dialogue, clichés are just part of the creation process. Just remember to cut them loose during self-editing.

There are two versions of clichés that are worth mentioning: **clichéd phrases and clichéd characters**. Let's review them in that order.

First, clichéd phrases are the *order of the day*. We want to *give them the bum's rush* to get our writing into *tip top shape*. Readers are not *rocking up* to read *old hat*. It's *boring as bat shit. You with me?* Banish the cliché to the banal corner of the world *from whence they came* … and use your own glorious words instead.

Second, clichéd characters are over before they start. These stereotypes follow a typical, predictable pattern. Consider the prostitute with the heart of gold, the absent-minded professor, the alcoholic priest, the wounded warrior, etc., and remember that this list is vast. If we do want to dip into this list, we need to ensure that our cliché develops his or her own characterisation to break through the stereotype and surprise the reader. Readers want that mix of cast members who are 'true to character' and 'make sense' coupled with the vast element of surprise.

Writers are alchemists and jugglers, forever trying to strike a fresh balance between the familiar and the unique. This task lies at the heart of crafting authentic phrases and characters.

Highlight Point of View

One edit should be devoted to observing POV. The perspective of the narrative should be consistent and clear. One 'earmark of the amateur' is a POV that shifts at random and confuses readers, also called head-hopping.

If the story's POV is shifted, it should have a good technical reason and be seamless, so readers won't stop to reread, wondering what they've missed. See Chapter Eight on POV for details, but for self-editing purposes, let's focus on some key points.

For works-in-progress, the POV might unconsciously change within a paragraph without any creative rationale, as we're still trying to find the best way to tell the story. For example, we might be speaking about us as writers (1st person plural) and then you as the writer (2nd person singular) then the writers (third person plural) all in one sentence, creating an unfocused result. For a cohesive short story, choose the POV and stick to it. Analyse the first draft, asking if the current POV is the best fit for this story.

- **For 1st person,** is this level of intimacy serving the narrative? Why does being inside the protagonist's head make the story more compelling?
- **For 2nd person,** does this semi-aggressive form of storytelling boss the reader around or does it have an appropriate immersive affect?
- **For 3rd person limited**, the most common POV for short fiction, are we limited to the right character? Does that character reward the reader's attention?
- **For 3rd person omniscient or objective,** is there a good reason to hover above the action and reveal character motives from a godlike view (omniscient)? If the narrator reads like hidden camera (objective) and does not impose any bias upon any of the characters or action, is the reader still confronted and surprised?

Don't be afraid to change the POV of a first draft to see how another might improve the storytelling. Experimentation can deepen a narrative from the original draft.

Next up in this edit, look for areas where POV is unintentionally sloppy, and stick to the dominant POV. A short story usually operates along one POV from start to finish.

The most common POV for short stories, as mentioned above, is 3rd person limited. If this is the dominant form, ensure that readers never experience the thoughts or emotions of any other characters unless through the lens of the protagonist. Here, the narrator is only privy to the interior world of the protagonist. Check each scene, as it's easy to 'head-hop' from one character to another, confusing the reader.

While it's unusual for short stories, 3rd person POV limited to dual or multiple characters can work. Just mark the changes in narration by a scene break, usually a double line space. Never allow a shift in POV within the same paragraph or scene, or the narrative is head-hopping.

The same rule goes for a 1st person narration. If 'I' am leading the narration, I can't tell the reader what the salesclerk is thinking. I have to report what I see and hear to the reader as an interpretation of the salesclerk's inner world. For example, I can't say in the narration that 'the salesclerk eyed me with anger', but I can say 'the salesclerk scowled at me'.

If 2nd person is the POV of the story, the entire piece is told from 'you'. You can tell the reader how 'you' think and feel but cannot describe the inner state of other characters. For example, the story can state, 'you jog past the kids on the beach who holler and laugh,' but cannot state, 'you jog past the kids on the beach who holler with happiness'. The 2nd person reports how that happiness is witnessed.

For a note on 'you'—sometimes 'you' drops into the prose by accident so do a document search for the word. A story in 1st or 3rd person POV can slip into 2nd even just for a sentence, as it's a conversational habit best left out of good prose. You know what I mean. I just did it.

Lastly, if we're playing with 3rd person omniscient, we must dip cautiously and with balance into characters' inner worlds. For objective, we don't dip into character interiors at all. The narrator stays either godlike or as a hidden camera, so revelations are compact or observed, respectively.

In general, ask these questions for this stage of a self-edit:

- Is the POV strategic and consistent?
- Is the POV limited to one character in each scene? Or are the inner thoughts of two characters shared in the same section?
- For the omniscient 3rd person POV, does the narrator oversee each scene from a godlike perspective? And does it dip into characters' interior experiences in a balanced way?
- For objective 3rd person POV, does the narrator maintain a specific distance from the characters like a hidden camera and simply report what is seen?
- If there are multiple or dual POV in this story, are there clear section breaks? Is the story strong enough to handle multiple POV, ensuing that each character who takes the lead is just as compelling as the others? Is there enough time devoted to each character to craft healthy, memorable characterisation?
- If 'you' slips into the prose, is it by accident? Can it be cut and replaced with the dominant POV?

Highlight Passive and Active Verbs

Is the writing predominantly active, not passive? There are two main areas to assess in terms of the active and passive: *verbs and characters*. Let's start with verbs.

Like telling, passive verbs litter first drafts. Stringy verb phrases that rely on the verb 'to be' like 'was' and 'were' and clunky writing that spans 'could', 'would', 'been', etc., is just a way to splash our stories onto the page. One early editing approach is to target these verbs and convert them to stronger, more active prose.

>**PASSIVE**: I **think our** friendship **grew stronger and we bonded**.
>**ACTIVE**: Our friendship strengthened.
>
>**PASSIVE**: Shelly ended up wearing the red dress.
>**ACTIVE**: Shelly wore the red dress.

Note how much more information we register as readers when sentences are articulated in the active voice, compared to the same in passive. Passive writing bores readers and lets their minds wander.

Verbs are the powerhouse of a sentence. Zero in on them and try to tighten up lines like this one:

>The doctor <u>was invited</u> by the captain
>to
>The captain <u>invited the doctor</u>.

This edit is simple. Tighten the verb and place the true subject of the sentence (the captain) first for a more ordered reading experience. Check drafts for compound verb phrases like 'was invited' and edit them to 'invited'.

To edit simple compound verbs that don't require much movement of the text, see this example:

The lion <u>was raging</u> at the crowd

to

The lion <u>raged</u> at the crowd.

Compound verb phrases like 'was raging', do not offer any reason for their presence but just creep into those early drafts. Instead make these verbs clear, precise and active. When we edit 2/3^{rds} of these in our stories, our writing increases in power.

Check out this example, another spin on the same concept:

The letter seemed to have come in on a gale

to

The letter swept in on a gale.

With editing, the above line is stronger for two reasons. First, we rid ourselves of that compound verb phrase, 'seemed to have come'. Second, we replace a banal verb, *come*, with a stronger, more colourful verb *swept*.

While it's great to edit most of these, there are occasions to use the passive voice and they span two reasons. One, we might use a passive verb phrase to sound passive, purposefully. There's a reason government writing prefers the phrase 'It was decided by the committee' over 'The committee decided' as it points to a deliberate tone of collaborative power.

Two, we might use a passive verb phrase for simultaneous action as in this example:

The siren was wailing as the door was jammed, might be a better fit for the dramatic action than *The siren wailed as the door jammed.*

We can see both lines as valuable within a scene, one crisper than the other. The former, however, illustrates the heightened tension involved with the two simultaneous actions.

Highlight Passive and Active Characters

Good characters make things happen. They don't simply react to what goes on around them. Readers—and publishers—want characters with agency.

During self-editing, we can apply a few measuring sticks to see where our characters stand. First, conduct a plot outline, which works well after the first draft is complete. Chart out the plot as it looks in the current draft to get a clear view of how the character arcs align with the narrative arc and assess how satisfying the experience is for readers. A plot outline also identifies any tangents or departures from the gravitational pull toward the climax, which will help locate ways to strengthen the cohesion of the story.

As the plot is mapped out, assess how characters respond to the events of the story through the following questions:

- At the start, did the central characters want something but they were blocked somehow? What are their obstacles and how to do they deal with them?
- Is there a question posed/an inciting incident at the start that is answered by the main character in the climax? Or does someone else take over? Good stories focus on that core question and core character, so let

the main character drive the climax ... not the sudden arrival of the cops.
- Does the main character make a promise to the reader at the start that is kept until the end? Is there a twist or surprise or some kind of wisdom shared?
- Do the characters act and respond to the events of the plot, or do they just go along with the current of the story?
- If the characters have agency and are responding to the plot points, are their actions authentic or cliché? Is it a bit tame, or does the character go far enough for good fiction? Remember that fiction is bold and tells the stories that need telling.
- If the main character is also the narrator through a 1st person point of view, is that voice active? Does the speaker make things happen?
- If the main character is an unreliable narrator who isn't always honest with the reader, is there some kind of payoff for the reader? A surprise? A challenge? A delicious level of discomfort?
- If the characters are passive, and truly need to be as it determines the theme, is there still payoff for readers? Is there a cost or a consequence of this passivity and is it strong enough?

Highlight Spelling and Grammar

We feel strongly about this. Serious writers are committed to learning exceptional spelling and grammar.

Sending a short story with mistakes into a competition diverts a portion of the judges' attention towards errors instead of the storyline; diluting the potency of the narrative in the judges' perspectives.

If the dream is to write a book, the more skills perfected early, the more money will be saved later. A polished piece of writing requires less time to edit, which will help manage the cost of hiring a book editor.

When sending writing to a professional editor, work that contains amateurish spelling, grammar and tense mistakes, diverts the editor's attention to fixing those errors. The writer misses out on the higher-level edit that a polished manuscript receives.

In other words, send an editor a poor manuscript, and they will make it good. Send an editor a good manuscript, and they will make it great. Send an editor an exceptional manuscript, and they will help achieve exquisite.

The more we self-edit, the better we get at it. Work matures and confidence is gained. Strengths and areas requiring skill development are identified.

Self-Edit Checklist

1. Map the story's structure and pace. Analyse.
2. Highlight adverb/verb combinations. Replace with strong verbs.
3. Look for filters and tautologies. Remove redundant words.
4. Rewrite information dumps. Scatter pieces of background info and description throughout action scenes.

5. Read dialogue out loud. Is it authentic and character nuanced?
6. Are the characters real? Active or passive? Do they have flaws? What change do they undergo in your story?
7. Mark sentences of *tell*. Rewrite to *show* if the information is important to the story.
8. Is point of view and tense consistent?
9. Highlight any clichés. Replace with original writing.
10. Is the spelling and grammar the best you can achieve?

Once self-edit cycles are complete and the story is the best the writer can achieve on their own, it's time to send the story to trusted, knowledgeable BETA readers for comment. The BETA reader relationships writers foster—having work read and critiqued by other writers and in exchange for reading and critiquing theirs—are a valuable tool in the writers' toolkit.

Not all writers have studied BETA reading, but we can nudge our BETA reader in the correct direction by asking a small number of targeted questions. For example, to demonstrate to a BETA reader that I want to know positive and negative feedback, and that I'm looking for *reactions* to my short story, not spellcheck, I might ask my BETA readers:

1. Mark sentences you found particularly delightful, and ones that grated on you.
2. What did you like about the story, and was there anything you disliked?

3. Were there any paragraphs you found boring, or not as interesting as the others?
4. What did you enjoy or not enjoy about the pace of the story?
5. Did the beginning grab you, and did the ending satisfy you? Describe, why/why not.
6. Did the lines of dialogue sound authentic?
7. What did you learn about the main character?
8. What did you think of the style of the writing?

The next chapter, Top Drawer Writing Groups and Peer Review, is a comprehensive database of minutiae to sharpen your BETA reading skills. We include it in this book to demonstrate the high value to a writer's development to be involved in a well-functioning writing/critique group.

CHAPTER TEN

TOP DRAWER WRITING GROUPS, AND PEER REVIEW

By L. E. Daniels

SOME of the most powerful tools in a writer's development are strong writing groups and targeted peer reviews. J.R.R. Tolkien, C.S. Lewis and Charles Williams called their group the Inklings at Oxford and trusted each other with sharpening their fantasy novels. The famous letters between Ernest Hemingway and F. Scott Fitzgerald also drove the authors to hone their craft. Hemingway told Fitzgerald, 'I liked it and I didn't…it's not as good as you can do' in 1934 when he read a draft of *Tender is the Night*. Despite the intense and sometimes combative nature of their connection, Fitzgerald still called Hemingway 'the greatest living writer of our time' and appreciated his insight.

Peer reviews and writing groups do two things for writers—new and established authors alike. They can…

- Provide good, evidence-based feedback on what works well and what needs development.
- Strengthen literary skills and powers of observation into what works and what doesn't work, first in another's writing—and *ultimately in our own.*
- Serve as a reminder that writing is a lifelong quest. Writers grow stronger and wiser when pushed to do their best.

Outside of actually writing, I don't think there's a better way to develop as a writer than to have colleagues who understand what we're trying to do. We can review each other's work in a positive, productive way and end up with stronger, more authentic prose. Writers can help each other see what's elusive in the writing process because there are formulas that work.

As many of us have experienced, fellow writers can be incredibly supportive or irreparably destructive. One good peer review can pry open a door on a previously locked up plot point or blow fresh energy into a closed character. It can show us problems we sensed in our stories but didn't precisely know where they were. One bad critique, however, can stab a manuscript to death. The work can be abandoned after such an attack, so caution and mutual respect are essential.

A good model with clear perimeters keeps the critique productive and respects the integrity of our creative process. A sound literary knowledge, which we can strengthen in the writing group, also ensures responses are as objective as possible and avoid creative wounding. Please see list of literary questions to explore when reviewing another writer's work at the end of this chapter, 'New to Critiquing? Try This'.

The following model works in a group setting for a writing group at home or the local library. It also works for a partnership, in person or remotely—emailing drafts and making notes via Microsoft Word's Track Changes function or Google Docs.

This critiquing model was instilled into my practice by several authors during my studies at Emerson College in Boston, Massachusetts, voted a top writing school in the USA in 2018 by *College Magazine* (11/09/2018). André Dubus III, author of the acclaimed novel, *House of Sand and Fog*, demonstrated the following values during my Master of Fine Arts studies and they have made me the editor, author and teacher I am today. These guidelines enable productive feedback as well as positive writing group proceedings while they uphold the integrity of the creative works-in-progress and protect the writer's individual process.

Everyone should emerge from their critique sessions inspired, not defeated. We want writers to leave sessions informed, excited and ready to engage their next round of edits.

Let's take this in stages.

When submitting a draft to a writing group or peer review, we want to…

- Identify the genre right there at the top of the writing sample so fellow writers know what to expect. Is it fiction or nonfiction? A personal essay, speculative fiction, children's, science fiction, etc.? Ensure the reader doesn't assess children's fiction as adult or fantasy as nonfiction.
- Note format and the audience, e.g., short story for women's magazine; chapter from young adult novel; short story for horror contest, etc., for clarity. Make a note if readers are reading just an excerpt.
- Cite specific areas we'd like our readers to note, e.g., 'Are the characters dimensional enough?' or 'Is the dialogue authentic for this age group?' or 'Is there enough setting?'
- Proofread and copyedit first. Read the sample aloud and spell check it. Format the dialogue in professional format. Errors detract from the quality of our feedback and distract readers from offering more helpful advice. While a few mistakes happen, we want quality prose to respect the reader's time and efforts.
- Use professional format accepted by publishers: size 12 Times New Roman font; 1.5 or double spaced and end the work with a ### rather than 'The End'. When our work gets accepted by a publisher, Times New Roman rolls smoothly into production software, while other fonts create errors, drop punctuation, or delete italics. Get the work to professional standard at

this stage so it's submission-ready when the time comes. Sometimes competitions can surprise us and we don't have much time to enter our work. This is one way to keep the process efficient.

When we hold another writer's draft in our hands, remember…

- **All work is in progress.** We're sensitive to the delicate nature of this process, the writer's nerves, and the temptation to defend the work, especially during critique.

- **Be open minded to genres outside our taste as potent learning tools.** If someone presents crime fiction and we don't normally read it, we have an opportunity to exercise objective, analytical muscles. We can observe what works and what presents opportunities for revision, further building our own writing skills. We can see and articulate how the technical aspects of writing orchestrate into art, regardless if we 'like' it. If we can separate ourselves from our opinions, we grow into quite a force in the writing world.

- **Track Changes or handwriting notes onto the piece using pencil/pen—no red pen, because it alarms some writers—are great approaches.** All copies are returned to writers for accountability and to give the writer a record to reference during revisions.

- **Note what works well.** No one wants a list of only everything that needs revision. Writers want to know where they're doing well, too. If we read something impressive, we praise it for its technical accuracy, poignancy, etc., and articulate the literary reason why it's good. Rather than reading a simple 'I like this' in a section, it's helpful for writers to read a note like 'Good adjective' or 'Vivid setting' or 'Clear action sequence here' or 'These short sentences convey tension'.

- **Use cautious, positive wording and provide evidence for observations.** If something is confusing or overwritten, show the writer where the text was confusing or bogged by details. If the story has dialogue that uses clichés, highlight a few. *Don't fix the problem or offer solutions but cite specific areas that need work and how it affected the reader.*

- **Avoid using the word 'you' in our review as a confrontational and even inaccurate word and instead cite the scene, the prose, the character, the plot, etc., in our comments.** Instead of 'You did a good job here with the setting details', we would write, 'These setting details evoke a sense of the 1970s'. Instead of writing 'Your ending falls flat', we would write, 'The ending needs development. Perhaps touch upon the theme?'

- **Lastly, and perhaps most important of all, *don't write the piece*.** This is tricky for writers, but essential. Write that the protagonist reads as two-dimensional and needs more development. Don't write that the answer is to make the protagonist a boxer. Write that the period piece needs more historical details to make the setting more complete. Don't write that the story needs cannons in the opening scene. This is so critical because once a reader crosses this line, the writer cannot uncross it and their creative process is contaminated. They have trouble forgetting about those darned cannons and even more trouble coming up with a creative solution of their own.

When the writing group meets...

- **Elect a moderator to create a sense of order and ensure speaking time is shared between members.** When breaches of the guidelines happen, the moderator can get the group back on track again.

- **Before the critique begins, a writer can address specific concerns about the work being critiqued.** This is the time to reiterate concerns about plot, character, etc., and ask that people offer comments in those areas.

- **Once the critique begins, the writer keeps silent unless asked a direct question for clarification.** It might sound pedantic, but a critique can quickly deteriorate into an attack/defend energy and this is one practical way to avoid catastrophe from the outset.

- **During the critique, group members discuss the work in turn while the writer takes notes.** This strategy ensures that everyone has a chance to speak and avoids creating a defensive situation.

- **During the critique, address the work, not the writer.** Again, avoid using the word 'you' when speaking, but instead refer to the piece, the character, etc. Trust me, this also prevents an argument.

- **Each reader cites what's working first before zeroing in on what needs work.** Let the writer know their strengths, which is just as important as the areas that need revision.

- **For the constructive criticism portion of the feedback, draw upon that cautious, positive wording used when the notes were compiled.** Use the language of suggestion and phrase feedback as rhetorical questions, e.g., 'What if...?' or 'I felt that the centre of the story lagged. What would happen if the conversations there were shorter?'

- **Be specific.** We cite pages, paragraphs and lines to support feedback.

- **Again, don't write the piece, even in conversation.** The moderator should stop a reader who veers into this territory, and it does happen. As mentioned above, creative solutions convolute an already complex process for the writer and can be sorely tempting for writers.

- **At the end of the critique, ask the writer to respond to the feedback, ask questions and receive clarification.** Get a sense of how the writer is feeling and ensure a supportive atmosphere. Give the writer a chance to voice any frustration or annoyance, if there is any as it's rare, and try to rectify it. At the end of the session, writers should feel inspired and equipped to revise their work.

New to Critiquing? Try This.

Feeling intimidated by the very idea of reading another writer's work and providing intelligent feedback? A little worried about this literary language and don't want to look stupid?

So is everyone else. It's terrifying, especially in a group setting, but it gets easier.

Here's a handy list to get you started and grow your confidence. As you read, try to observe the writing across the following literary categories. Eventually, you'll apply this lens to your own work as you self-edit, so it's win-win.

Identify the angle or theme of the story you're reading for the critique. The angle is the theme/core message that can be summed up in a phrase in a working draft. It could be in the title, such as 'Alien in My Cupboard', or within the prose itself, such as 'unrequited young love'.

- Can you sum up the theme in one sentence? Is it apparent? Or buried?
- If there is more than one theme, does the piece succeed in delivering all the angles clearly or do they get muddled? Can you identify why?
- Does a theme or two need to be pared away to strengthen the central theme?

Observe the narrative arc—the storyline—and ask if all the parts contribute to the narrative and support the angle. The movement of the narrative arc determines whether a story lingers or moves at a healthy clip. It also reflects the trajectory toward the climax and the cohesion of the piece.

- Do any sections support/propel the angle or pull away and become tangents?
- Do any thoughts feel incomplete or leave you wanting more?
- Do you feel 'left out' and confused anywhere?
- What needs further development to help readers fully grasp what is at stake?
- What feels repetitive/drawn out and needs tightening?

Identify the core conflict driving the story.

- What do the characters want/need? Is it clear?
- Are there obstacles in their way? Does this affect the pace and create tension?

Identify the plot and the plot points which compose the narrative arc. Remember, plot is action, e.g.,
1. Giges kills the king; 2. Giges marries the queen; and 3. Giges becomes king of Lydia for 30 years.

- What events and changes occur in the piece? Are they believable or over the top?
- What do the players [speaker/characters] learn or come to understand?
- What is the climax? Is there an inciting incident at the start that asks a question that will be answered at the climax?
- Is there a discernible arc of rising action → climax → falling action/denouement?

Question where the story starts and how the story ends.

- Is there a hook at the start that draws the reader in?
- Is there 'throat clearing' at the start, where it reads like the writer is 'warming up'?
- Can the story start later/sooner? End sooner/later?

- Is the ending earned? Does it reflect the theme? Is there a true sense of conclusion or does it need development?

Consider the structure.

- Can the writer consider alternatives from straight chronology, such as the frame?
- Observe the transitions. Do scenes move along cleanly or do elements jar/confuse readers?
- Observe the flow from paragraph to paragraph. Do you ever have to stop and reread to figure out what's happening?

Consider the characters and setting.

- Can you see, hear and imagine the characters and setting? Are you shown more than told about the cast and the environment?
- Are they fleshed out or flat? Are they real and alive?
- Are there big chunky paragraphs that catalogue their details or are the details woven through the scenes and action?
- Do the characters provoke a reaction from you? Could they use further development?
- Is there a strong setting/sense of place revealed through the senses?

- Are there clear character arcs (growth, shift, change, or fall arcs) or are they static? Do they read as authentic or clichéd? Are there surprises or are they predictable?

Assess the dialogue.

- Does each moment of dialogue underscore the conflict, drive the plot, and develop the theme?
- Do any moments of dialogue need cutting, expanding or editing?
- Is dialogue used as an 'info dump' where a character talks out the exposition and details the world in an obvious, inauthentic way?
- If any clichés are used, do they shed light on the characters and their backgrounds? Or are the clichés just boring and unconscious?
- Are there too many or scarce stage directions/physical details? Are they overwritten or do the conversations read like disembodied voices?
- Can you see the setting where the cast are conversing or is it a white space?
- Are there adverbs in the dialogue that sound false, like 'she asked quizzically'?
- Is the dialogue attribution simple, and therefore more invisible to readers (said, asked, shouted) or are they distracting (retorted, chuckled, squealed)?

- Do characters sound similar to one another or are their voices so cultivated and unique that you can tell them apart without the dialogue attribution?

Overall, are you shown more than you are told?

- Does the writer use all of the senses? Auditory, visual, kinetic, olfactory, tactile?
- Are there an array of literary devices used, like foreshadow, symbolism and motif, to communicate the theme and tighten the structure?
- Are there fleshed out scenes that bring the story alive?
- Are there adverbs that tell more than they show and can be cut?
- Did you find yourself 'skipping' over sections because they are telling or were you riveted?
- Are there any places where you feel a scene is untold, waiting to be crafted?
- Are there long sections of exposition that could be trimmed or peppered more through the scene?

Consider the voice and tone of the piece.

- Is the voice strong and developed or does it falter in places? Is it intimate or distant? Trustworthy or unreliable? Why?
- Are there clichés? Are there places of original writing?

- Does the mood/emotional texture suit the piece? Are there tonal details that support the piece or are there anachronisms—details/phrases/terms) that do not match the time period/culture?
- Is there a bias/opinion that distances the speaker from readers? Is it preachy or didactic? How so?
- Is every observation backed by some kind of tangible, sensory evidence?
- Are there places where the piece could delve a little deeper and give the narration a more authentic presence?

Identify the perspective/point of view [POV] of the piece. Point of view takes practise to assess, so be gentle with yourself.

- If the story is in the 1st person POV (I), does this POV offer a deep intimacy between the speaker/protagonist and the reader? Are there revelations? Is it engaging or does the speaker need more depth?
- If the story is told from the 2nd person POV (you), is it powerful or irritating? Is there a clear reason why the story works in this form?
- If the story is told in 1st or 3rd person POV, does the use of 'you' come and go with the direct purpose of drawing the reader into the story? Or is it sporadic, informal, and used in an unconscious conversational style? Does the speaker use 'you' when the action or

content gets emotionally intense, and disrupt the intensity?
- Is it in the 3rd person POV [he, she, they]? Is the POV limited to one character or does the narrator follow multiple characters? If we are limited to one character, can we only hear this protagonist's thoughts/feelings or do we head-hop into other characters' thoughts/feelings by accident?
- If we are 3rd person POV limited to dual or multiple characters, are there section breaks to indicate a change to the character the narrator is following closely? Or are we head-hopping from one character to another?
- Lastly, is this story in the 3rd person POV omniscient or objective? If omniscient, we should have a godlike narrator who watches characters from a distance or reveals their interior in a balanced, economical way. Is this consistent? For objective, does a removed, unbiased observer—like a hidden camera—consistently serve the story and the theme, reveal only what it can see, and stay out of people's heads?

Copyediting. Observe the paragraph and sentence structure, the verb phrases and verb tense.

- Are there powerful sentences that strike you?
- Are there some that are distracting because they are flowery [purple prose], clunky [awkward], or over the top?

- Are there repetitive, redundant words or filters in the prose?
- Is there adjective overload? Or is there just the right amount of descriptors?
- Is the tense all in the past or the present? Or does it jump around? Is the verb tense appropriate or distracting? Can you see a reason for the chosen tense?
- Are there many verb phrases and usages of could have, should, had, has, been, seem, and the clunky verb 'to be' (is, was, were, will) instead of more powerful, active, single-word verbs?
- Are sentence length and paragraph length varied? Are there any sentences or paragraphs that are just too long?
- Are there too many rhetorical questions? Often, these act as scaffolding for story drafts and can be removed as a draft develops.
- Do short sentences convey stress and tension? Is there a rhythm and flow to the prose? How do some parts sound read aloud?

Yes, it's a tremendous amount to absorb—another reason writing groups and peer reviews are so powerful in nurturing and developing your craft. You get to experiment. You get to make mistakes. You get to fix them. And you'll learn so much every time you try.

All the while, you'll apply the terminology an editor or publisher will use when your work is accepted for publication.

And you want to be well oiled when that time comes, so you know precisely what they're asking of you and you can deliver.

Which leads us to the last chapter in *Winning Short Story Competitions*—Your Title, Your Promise. I'm sure most will agree, at times spectacular titles seem to fall gloriously upon us from out of the sky. But what to do when they don't?

CHAPTER ELEVEN

YOUR TITLE, YOUR PROMISE

By C. Sawyer & L. E. Daniels

YOUR title creates anticipation and expectation, or conversely, disinterest. That's a mountain of pressure to place on a few words.

Ernest Hemingway tried out two prior titles before landing on *A Farewell to Arms* for what went on to become his first bestseller. It was originally 'The World's Room' and then 'They Who Get Shot'. Titles are subjective and resonate differently with different readers. And even Hemingway, a master, struggled with this process too.

With years of experience working with writers angsting over titles, my big tip is to have a little fun—if there's one thing I've witnessed, it's that relaxed writers with a twinkle in their eye most often come up with the best titles.

However, if that's not working, mull over this:

Great titles tend to have strong verbs, inherent conflict, character names, place names, poetic language or a quirky factor.

Strong verbs elicit power, which subconsciously draw a potential reader's interest.

Conflict elicits mystery, and who amongst us can resist the temptation?

Character names feel personal—connection is the main driver of human existence.

Place names elicit memory, fondness or desire by those who recognise them.

Poetic language is hypnotic.

And the quirky factor—when a browsing reader asks, 'What the?' … most can't resist completing that sentence.

Pick one of the above and you're on the winning track.

Your title is your promise. Be authentic—choose a title that promises what it delivers. If there's one thing that'll birth bad reviews— it's a dissatisfied reader. False promises backfire.

Lauren's Quick Tip on Titles

I've seen radiant titles fall from the sky onto writers, myself included, with no effort at all. Other times—maybe most times—we have to beg and bargain with the muse and still get silence. And deadlines might be pushing for that title, so we still have to act.

When we're stuck, theme is my first port of call. I go there and take the authors I support there too. If we're having trouble finding the title—I say finding, because I think it's always there somewhere, intact, like something submerged in the sand of our creative process—we retrace our steps and remember our theme, plug into it, feel it wash over us and the answer will come. We reconnect with our drive to write the story in the first place. We go deep and swirl in the chaos of the right brain and all the emotions that compel us to write fiction and try to understand our experiences. We seek that angel we've been wrestling all along and sometimes we find it standing right there, gleaming.

Another place to visit is the imagery. Do we have a motif—a recurring item, colour, phrase/saying, or action that builds and changes through the story until it delivers, in its final appearance, a humming resonance, like a tuning fork, with the core theme? Are there symbols that rise repeatedly from the story to convey its very heart to readers?

The answer always comes. It might look like a messy whiteboard or a raging mind-map octopus at first, but the answer always comes.

Sleep on it.

Ask the muse again.

And again.

Remember what drove us to write this story in the first place and how we hung pictures all over it. Remember that we write to say the things most people can't and look for the common ground.

Writing is an act of trust. We believe the words will come and eventually, they do. The same goes for your title. Keep asking until it arrives and you'll know it's the one.

RECOMMENDED RESOURCES

Books

Bell, James Scott. *Plot & Structure*. Writers Digest Books, Cincinnati, Ohio: 2004.

Cron, Lisa. *Wired for Story: The Writer's Guide to Using Brain Science to Hook Readers from the Very First Sentence*. Ten Speed Press, Berkeley, CA: 2012.

Cresswell, Julia. *The Penguin Dictionary of Clichés*. Penguin, NY: 2000.

King, Stephen. *On Writing*. Scribner: 2000.

Lamott, Anne. *Bird by Bird*. Anchor Books, Random House, NY: 1995.

Moffett, James & Kenneth R. McElheny. *Points of View: An Anthology of Short Stories, Revised Ed.* Mentor, Penguin, NY: 1995.

Puglisi & Ackerman. *The Emotion Thesaurus: A Writer's Guide to Character Expression.* 2nd Edition: 2019.

Solomon, Barbara H. *Other Voices, Other Vistas: A Superb Collection of Contemporary Multi-Cultural Fiction.* Mentor, Penguin, NY: 1992.

Strunk, William & E.B. White. *The Elements of Style.* Harcourt, NY: 1920.

Style Manual for Authors, Editors & Printers, 6th Ed. Wiley & Sons, Canberra: 2002.

Wood, James. *How Fiction Works.* Farrar, Straus & Giroux, NY: 2008.

Websites: For great stories, tips & submission calls

Anton Chekhov Free Short Stories: http://www.free-short-stories.org.uk/anton-chekhov-free-short-stories.htm

Hawkeye Books: https://hawkeyebooks.com.au/ for the Sydney Hammond Memorial Short Story Competition, the Hawkeye Publishing Manuscript Development Prize, and news articles.

Hawkeye Publishing: https://hawkeyepublishing.com.au/submission calls.

Plays to Read to Improve Your Story's Dialogue: https://medium.com/@writersrelief/writers-plays-to-read-to-improve-your-storys-dialogue-b1951667730f

Poets & Writers: https://www.pw.org/

Short Stories Everyone Should Read: https://www.esquire.com/uk/culture/books/g15840493/best-short-story-collections-books/

Short Story Guide, Best Australian Short Stories: http://www.shortstoryguide.com/australian-short-stories/

Writers Digest: https://www.writersdigest.com/

Podcasts: Dig into these archives for global voices

Best Australian Podcasts: https://www.techradar.com/au/best/the-best-australian-podcasts

Fifteen Short Story Podcasts: https://blog.feedspot.com/short_story_podcasts/

Selected Shorts: https://www.symphonyspace.org/selected-shorts

Ten Storytelling Podcasts: https://www.bustle.com/p/10-storytelling-podcasts-you-need-to-listen-to-if-you-love-short-stories-15566864

The New Yorker Fiction Podcast: https://www.newyorker.com/podcast/fiction

TEN WEEKS OF CREATIVE WRITING EXERCISES TO HONE YOUR SKILLS

THE following exercises are designed to give you ten weeks of exploration, targeting one specific literary skill at a time, as covered by this book.

Have fun with these and get a writing partner if you can so you can practice the critiquing skills in this book as well. You can even incorporate these exercises into a writing group and make them—and their creative results—part of your discussion.

Experiment and enjoy! And at the end of ten weeks, you'll have mastered some new skills.

WEEK ONE: Show More than Tell

Let's practise this core skill, as even established authors slip into 'telling' just to get that first draft out. The trick is to convert a good portion of 'telling' into 'showing' to create engaging scenes.

Refer to chapter – Hint, Tantalise, Reel Me In – for devices used by the skilled writer to capture the elements of dramatisation. Then, try converting these 'telling' sentences into moments that 'show' the reader a scene. Use some of the advice from the chapter and experiment.

You can develop the idea into paragraphs that are fictional and connect to a story you're writing, or you can draw directly from your own experiences. You can change them to suit your content. You can do one or all of them.

1.) I was angry.
2.) The view was magnificent.
3.) I swam in cold (or warm) water.
4.) It was an interesting event.
5.) The musical was boring.
6.) It was the worst (or best) day ever.
7.) I envied him.
8.) It's complicated.
9.) No one has ever been sadder than that man.
10.) It's a great time to be alive.

WEEK TWO: Dialogue that Shows More than Tells

Refresh your mind with the content from chapter – BFFs: How Dialogue Makes Plot, Theme & Conflict Shine. Then, try to first sketch out a moment of tension between two characters just by telling it. You can try these as springboards:
1. Person A and Person B discuss a problem. One of them is lying and the other one knows it.

2. Persons A and B just had an argument but have to reconcile because they both need the same thing or to share something.
3. Persons A and B are dear friends or have been married for decades. They forgive each other daily for the other's shortcomings.
4. A is the parent and B is the child. A is trying to teach B to try something new and B doesn't want a bar of it, at first.

First, write it all out to tell it and get the story down. If I use example 2, my draft would look like: *A walks into the kitchen and is angry because B is already using the last of the eggs to make an omelette. A thinks this is typical. A starts banging around the kitchen. B notices but keeps cooking and chatting, oblivious to the reason for A's anger. B asks A to go cut some parsley from the garden. A swears all the way there and back to the kitchen, a fistful of the herb in her hand. B chops parsley and sprinkles it into the omelette. B cuts the omelette in half and serves it to A. A is sorry and sick of self isolation.*

Then I would convert parts of this telling to dialogue and scene detail for more dramatic effect.

WEEK THREE: Show More Than Tell: Omitting Sensing Verbs [Filters]

More than anything else, writers want to draw readers into the story. We want readers to forget they're reading and to experience our stories unfolding within their own minds like a dream. There are a multitude of ways to cultivate this effect for readers and just as many ways to, well ... wake them up. Let's explore a common one.

Sensing verbs, also called 'filters', are essential to getting the story out of our heads and onto the page, but sometimes they stick around in a draft when they can be culled by self-editing. Filters distance a reader from the action and make the reader more aware of the fact that they are reading. To see what I mean, consider the difference between these two pairs:

> He stood at the window and saw a storm rolling towards the island.
>
> He stood at the window. A storm rolled towards the island.
>
> I knew the water was freezing and felt it sear my feet. The icy water stung my feet.

The latter examples draw readers into the action, allowing them to experience the situation. The former read like first drafts that are still trying to nut out what's happening.

Let's play with this idea of filters, showing & telling.

Step 1: Read through a sample of your writing and circle every word that explains one of the five senses. Phrases like, 'I heard', 'I felt', and 'I smelled' are weak. They tell rather than show and force readers further away from the experience.

Step 2: Replace filters with specific, strong verbs and other sensations. If you heard someone coming up behind you, how did you hear it? Was it crunching on gravel or padding on tiles? Was it the shuffling against carpet? Every edit here is an opportunity to upgrade your writing.

Editing Examples: Edit these for filters and telling words. Rewrite and continue if you want to use them as prompts.

1. As I turned the key in the lock, I heard footsteps rush up behind me. I felt a rush of adrenaline as I turned and I saw an enormous dog bounding my way.
2. She stepped from her car and looked to a valley of lush grass. She saw what a week of rain had finally done to the place. It was magical.
3. He smelled smoke and began to cough, drawing his elbow over his mouth and nose. When he opened the kitchen door, he saw two teenagers burning their homework sheets in the sink and heard the fire alarms start to wail.

How would you change these without forcing your readers to see through a filter?

WEEK FOUR: Motif

Let's take a break from the old showing and telling exercises and play with motif. One of the most common issues with an early draft is a lack of focus or a diffused centre of gravity.

Motif is a superb way to enhance the cohesion of a short story and it's a lot of fun to write. I believe it's so satisfying because it draws on a writer's natural ability to form unusual connections and craft that 'hall of mirrors' that makes good stories great.

First, let's review what a motif is, so you know how to grow them in your stories. Motif is a recurring image that forms a pattern in a story and builds, so that by the end of the story, the image conveys the deepest themes of the story. Some examples of motif are:

Items: Harry Potter's scar points to his destiny and the power of love.

Colour: Light and dark in Joseph Conrad's *Heart of Darkness* plays on knowledge and ignorance; life and death, etc.

Concepts/Phrases: Freedom is engaged and discussed in dialogue, narration, and on many levels in Margaret Atwood's *The Handmaid's Tale*.

Action: The wife's preparation of a frozen leg of lamb in the short story, 'Lamb to the Slaughter' by Roald Dahl reflects a mix of a homemaker's duties with murder.

Mood: The gloomy, haunted settings of Harper Lee's *To Kill a Mockingbird* reflect the coexistence of good and evil in one small town.

Characters: A silent witness may appear several times in a story as an extension of the reader. An aging person may represent wisdom or death. A youth may represent vitality. The key for motif as character lies in repeated appearances alongside a deepening of the theme. Consider the witches in Shakespeare's *Macbeth* and how each time they appear or are referenced, Macbeth's world has fallen more deeply into chaos.

Let's reflect on a story you're working on, one you want to write. Consider an image you've observed in your story idea or even in your life. Do you see how that recurring image can point to and even develop the theme you want to write about?

Place the story itself aside for a moment and write about that recurring image in a set of three, with each of the three moments building upon the last and changing.

For an easy example, I might choose water as a symbol for life. Perhaps in my first sketch, water can be shown as something that drowns; in my second, it might be shown as something that carries someone home; and in my third, it might be shown as something that cleanses and refreshes the landscape. Sketch out the same with yours, with a clear sense of progression.

The goal is to flesh out your motif; to tease out how this 'thing' can connect with your deeper theme; then to lace it with the old cut and paste, into your working draft at the right spots.

Think of it as placing flowers or hanging pictures in a home—in just the right spot.

WEEK FIVE: Show Don't Tell, But Tell Sometimes

The big writing rule is always show don't tell, but more accurately, it should be: we show most of the time and when we tell, we tell strategically.

Telling the reader something is like using a short cut. Before or after descriptive writing, a direct line of telling can be very dramatic like 'I had a farm in Africa' or 'It was the best of times, it was the worst of times' or 'It was a pleasure to burn' or 'Mother died today' or 'Everything was beautiful and nothing hurt'.

For an example of how telling can work for you, imagine a colourful description of a man looking out from the window of a rotten old house, gazing out at a blackening sea. See the dark clouds cloaking the sunset and the empty, stony beach lined with beach grass and thorny brambles. We let the prose light upon a lonely fishing trawler chugging towards the decrepit marina and a solitary seagull preening on a post. Then end the paragraph with a line like, *No moon rises over this haunted place. He is all alone and terrified.*

That's showing punctuated by the blow of telling in the right spot, to accentuate a mood, but it does not rely upon telling to drive the story.

For our exercise, let's pair a tone with a character and place this person into a setting. It can be a fictional character or ourselves, if we're into memoir. It can be like the example above—fear with a man alone in a haunted place … or it could be any of these:

- Love between a couple in a foreign country.
- Anxiety of a child lost in a strange place.
- Joy of a parent of a newborn in the quiet corner of a busy hospital.
- Grief for a pet owner home alone for the first time in years.
- Anticipation at a reunion away from home.

Choose one or come up with your own and…

1. Place the speaker or character within the setting/scene;

2. Explore the setting through the lens of emotion to set the tone but do not label the emotion (the fishing boat can be lonely, for example, but not the man); and
3. End with a short, sharp statement of telling that broadcasts an element of the scene and adds one more bit of information (like the house is haunted).

Have fun. Stretch your muscles. Overwrite and blow out the description then edit to tighten it. Jig and rejig that final line that tells the reader something directly.

WEEK SIX: Why the 'Road to Hell is Paved with Adverbs' ~Stephen King

Adverbs can serve as 'short cuts' in prose and speed things up in the storytelling. *He fell awkwardly* is faster to read, for example, than *He fell over the dog into the trash can.*

Sometimes we want to pick up the pace and skip through a sequence. Sometimes we don't. We need, as writers, to make these choices with a clear sense of purpose.

When we use adverbs, we might lose the details that help compose a scene. Falling awkwardly means a lot of different things to a lot of different people. If how he falls and what he falls into matter to the story, we need to slow down a little and show it to readers.

Let's write badly first, in order to write consciously later.

First, write a paragraph with as many adverbs (verb modifiers that mostly end in 'ly' but not always like sometimes, often, always) as possible. Describe an incident when someone behaved foolishly or in anger. Show someone driving like a maniac or doing something tremendously selfish or show a person about to make a mistake. Stories with an emotional charge can be easier—and more fun—for this exercise.

Read your writing aloud when you're done. It should sound glaring and even funny.

Then take all the adverbs away and replace them with imagery (like falling over a dog and into a trash can). Compare the two.

In short, not all adverbs are bad. They serve a purpose at times. Try to be aware of them and to cull them as you edit for stronger, more vivid prose. Use adverbs consciously and ensure that they serve your story, not weaken it.

WEEK SEVEN: Symbolic Links: Allusion & Metaphor

Allusion and metaphor are two sub-categories of symbolism. They add a resonant layer to fiction that amplifies the message, both consciously and subconsciously for readers. These can come so naturally to some writers while others, who may be more inclined to concrete thinking, can struggle.

If you're shaky on these literary terms, let's consider a few famous examples before we play.

Allusion

A reference to a person, place, thing, event, that echoes with theme, action or character within a work. It works like a short cut in a story, drawing the qualities of something the reader knows into the narrative without taking the time to explain it.

Herman Melville named the ship, *Pequod*, in Moby Dick, alluding to New England's Pequot War (1636-1637). The bloody conflict between colonials and the local Indigenous population weighed on the minds of Melville's readers and resonated with the pursuit, violence and killing that drives this narrative.

In *Hamlet*, Act 3, Scene 4, the title character alludes to three Greek gods as he describes a portrait of his late father. He cites Hyperion's curly hair, Jove's prominent forehead, and Mars, god of war. The allusion conveys insight about the father of Hamlet.

> See what a grade was seated on this brow,
> Hyperion's curls, the front of Jove himself,
> An eye like Mars' to threaten and command...

Metaphor

An implied or hidden comparison between two unrelated things that have one or more parallels. Let's see a few, that explore different aspects of a story:

- **Characterisation:** 'Her mouth was a fountain of delight.'
  —*The Storm*, Kate Chopin.

- **Relationships that surround the protagonist:** 'The parents looked upon Matilda in particular as nothing more than a scab. A scab is something you have to put up with until the time comes when you can pick it off and flick it away.'
  —*Matilda*, Roald Dahl.

- **Complex concept:** 'My thoughts are stars I cannot fathom into constellations.'
  —*Fault In Our Stars,* John Green.

- **Action with symbolic quality:** 'Sit down, Montag. Watch. Delicately, like the petals of a flower. Light the first page, light the second page. Each becomes a black butterfly. Beautiful, eh? Light the third page from the second and so on, chain-smoking, chapter by chapter, all the silly things the words mean, all the false promises, all the second-hand notions and time-worn philosophies.'
  —*Fahrenheit 451,* Ray Bradbury.

For an exercise, pull up one of your works-in-progress. Do you see an opportunity to deepen what you've written through allusion or metaphor?

Opportunities can be missed here, so investing a little more energy at the editing level can push a story right over the line into the winner's circle.

Ask yourself these questions:

- **Allusion:** Are there are any events, items, names—either contemporary to the story's time line or timeless like mythology or art—that convey an echo of your theme?

- **Metaphor:** Can one of the characters, events, or concepts in your story allow for more colourful language? Is there a comparison to be made to amplify the point you're trying to make for readers?

Have fun exploring your draft and looking for opportunities. Adding this layer to your work is as satisfying as placing black butterflies among burning pages, conjuring Roman gods, or naming a ship.

WEEK EIGHT: An Alternative Structure: Practicing *in medias res*

The first mode of our storytelling is usually chronological order. In our draft, we might start at the start and work from there. This week, let's challenge our approach with *in medias res*, or the classical technique of starting in the middle of the story to amplify the dramatic action and hook our readers.

Let's draft up or pull out a draft of a short story. Identify the plot points including the climax/climactic revelation and resolution.

See these plot points for an example:

1. Alison travels to a farm stay. Her son, the youngest of her three, has left home and she's sad. She says goodbye to her husband for the weekend. [exposition]
2. Alison meets the friendly couple who walk the property with her and show her the animals, then to her room. She unwinds with a bath. [rising action]
3. A knock at the door in the early evening. A mare is giving birth and she's invited to the barn. [rising action]

4. She watches as a colt is born and is surprised by her quiet tears and memories of the birth of her son. [climax]
5. Alison stays with the mare and the foal until sunrise. Exhausted and honoured by the experience, she feels her sadness lifted. [resolution]

What if we began the story with #3, the knock at the door in the early evening? Then we moved to #1, #2, just referenced #3 before moving right into #4 and #5? That would be an easy way to amplify the action and would be using in medias res as a way to hook the reader.

If you wanted to try another variation, the frame, you can start and end the story with #5, and start with the setting accompanied with just a hint of the satisfaction and release that is to come.

WEEK NINE: Writing from the Dreamlike State

Let's freewrite. And I mean really freewrite. Freewrite like a freefall into your story.

To freewrite is to just run with it, to write without thinking or editing or trying to sound smart or original or any of it. You write to hit that vein and let it flow without any regard for how it sounds.

Author Richard Bausch wrote, 'If you think that you are thinking when you're writing, think again.' Can you allow yourself to lie fallow in that space, and to receive strokes of wonder?

Give it a try. Don't read what you're writing, just relax and follow the words.

Some prompts might be:
I wish I had a...
I never told anyone this, but this is what it really feels like when...
Maybe I wasn't clear when I said...
At the edge of the world, I see...

Maybe, if you're working on a specific story, you can just drop into a scene that you are trying so hard to write by thinking your way around it and instead, drop into the dream and try again...

When you are ready to reread, maybe 90% will be compost, bones, and moss, but I promise, there will be gold in there.

WEEK TEN: Point of View (POV)

As we explored in Chapter Eight, one of the more challenging technical aspects of creative writing is point of view. So let's play with it. Try telling the same story from these four basic forms of POV, with descriptions below.

1st person POV
2nd person POV
3rd person limited POV
3rd person omniscient or objective POV

Choose a prompt from one of the following or use your own.
- A wedding ceremony from the POV of the bride, the groom, a grandparent, a waiter, or anyone else.

- An argument in a grocery store between a cashier and a customer.
- A family suspects their old Queenslander is haunted.
- A couple rents a sailboat at the Whitsundays and something breaks.
- A tree falls in one neighbour's yard and falls on another neighbour's house.

In 1st person POV, the POV comes directly from the narrator. Readers know the interior thoughts and feelings of the main character (protagonist) only as the story unfolds. Choose one of the characters and tell that story from their perspective.

In 2nd person POV, 'you' are the star of the story. Write the story in the imperative voice. Google 'imperative voice' if you're not sure what that means.

In 3rd person limited POV, the narrator tells the story limited to the bride, for example, and can share her thoughts but the narrator can only report what she sees. If the narrator wants to report how the grandmother is feeling, we need to experience it through the observations of the bride.

In 3rd person omniscient or objective POV, has two forms—the narrator tells the story from 1.) a godlike perspective that is omniscient or 2.) from a hidden camera perspective. For omniscient, we might tap into various characters' thoughts, but we don't go too deeply and keep it balanced. Try not to head-hop. Alternatively as a hidden camera for objective, we stay out of characters' minds and just show everyone from the outside. We let their observable actions tell us who they are.

Play around with this as much as you'd like and you'll master it. You'll begin to feel instinctively which POV best serve the stories you want to tell.

THE AUTHORS THANK:

Brisbane Writers Workshop for its generosity in allowing us to include L. E. Daniels' *Ten Weeks of Creative Writing Exercises to Hone Your Skills*. brisbanewriters.com.

Christine Johnson, prize-winning author.

C. T. Mitchell, author of the international bestselling Jack Creed mystery series. ctmitchellbooks.com

Davide A. Cottone, author of *Shriek* & *Vietnam … Viet Bloody Nam*. piebooks.net

Diane Clarke author, dianeclarkeauthor.com

Geneve Flynn, author and editor geneveflynn.com.au

Hawkeye Publishing for its generosity in re-printing Christine Johnson's story from *Allsorts: Stories from under the Southern Cross*. 2019. hawkeyebooks.com.au.

Sign up to the newsletter at hawkeyebooks.com.au
to receive news of the authors' latest releases.

Coming soon from L. E. Daniels & C. Sawyer …
Writing Memoirs & Family Histories: Crafting Lives into Stories.

Other books by C. Sawyer & L. E. Daniels
available at hawkeyebooks.com.au:

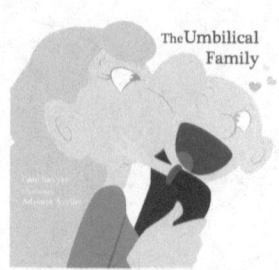

Cate Sawyer's picture books are phonics based and designed to create an early love for reading. *Discombobulated* is highly recommended by a Teacher Librarian specialising in gifted children. *Pelican't Do It* is particularly popular with parents of siblings because it touches on jealousy in a positive light. *It's Raining Shoes* explores imaginative play. *The Umbilical Family* honours family diversity: adoption, fostering, IVF, step parenting and grandparents.
And *Places to Poop* is LOVED by kids.

Lauren Daniels' *Serpents Wake: a Tale for the Bitten* is an exemplar of show not tell fiction writing as referenced in *Winning Short Story Competitions*.

Sydney Hammond Memorial Short Story Competition

Who was Syd Hammond?

Syd Hammond appeared to be like any ordinary guy. But those who loved him, knew different. He was so much more than ordinary. Syd was born in 1937 and died in 2007, aged 70. As a teenager he taught himself to play guitar. When rock-n-roll first sounded on radio there wasn't sheet music to follow. Syd and his mates crowded into booths at record stores. They listened keenly to identify their instruments. He hand-made his first electric guitar. He was one of the first Brisbane musicians to play music on TV.

In 1964, Syd received a bravery award for capturing one of Queensland's most wanted criminals – Bernard Morrow. Driving in his police patrol car, Syd noticed a drunk driver. He pulled him over, and casually suggested the gent go to the police station to sleep it off before he drove any further. Bernard Morrow complied. At the station, with Bernard sleeping it off, Syd sat at a desk and a WANTED poster caught his eye. Staring back at him were the eyes of the man already locked in the cell. He orated with glee the story of luck getting him a bravery award.

Syd portrayed a quintessential Aussie spirit of larrikin, 'give it a go, mate', mateship, and do the best you can for your family.

Syd loved Australia. He believed in standing up for what you believe in. He believed that music, art, humour and stories are the drumbeats that bring people together.

Tragedy struck in 2000 when his daughter, Julie, and son-in-law, John, were murdered by an intruder. The grief and injustice ran deep. When tragedy strikes we're reminded of what really matters in our lives. When families are so harmed they often look to transform their heartbreak into community support for others to find the positive.

The Sydney Hammond Memorial Short Story Competition to honour his memory was founded by his family.

For Carolyn, Syd's daughter and the Director of Hawkeye Publishing, words are held with reverence. The ability to articulate to be meaningful, thought-provoking and entertaining fosters community, understanding, change, healing, celebrating all that should not be taken for granted.

Words are powerful, and our wish with this competition is to acknowledge talented wordsmiths and give writers the opportunity to be heard.

The competition is not-for-profit—profit from the year before is used as the following year's prize money. Judges announce the winner, short-list and long-list. The top 40 stories are published in an anthology, and all those published receive a free copy of the book. **Guidelines and entry form can be found at www.hawkeyebooks.com.au.**

Hawkeye Publishing thanks the inaugural sponsors who made the competition possible: Tony & Christine Hammond (gold sponsors), Lynette Hammond, and Shane & Karen Traversari. We also thank our current gold sponsor: Brisbane Writers Workshop.

The Hawkeye Team

Hawkeye Publishing highly recommends Brisbane Writers Workshop for short writing courses. Go to www.brisbanewriters.com.

www.ingramcontent.com/pod-product-compliance
Lightning Source LLC
Chambersburg PA
CBHW011150290426
44109CB00025B/2560